Series/Number 07-131

MULTIPLE AND GENERALIZED NONPARAMETRIC REGRESSION

D0165411

JOHN FOX
McMaster University

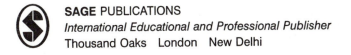

SAGE PUBLICATIONS
International Educational and Professional Publisher
Thousand Oaks London New Delhi

For information:

Sage Publications, Inc.
2455 Teller Road
Thousand Oaks, California 91320
E-mail: order@sagepub.com

Sage Publications Ltd.
6 Bonhill Street
London EC2A 4PU
United Kingdom

Sage Publications India Pvt. Ltd.
M-32 Market
Greater Kailash I
New Delhi 110 048 India

Printed in the United States of America

Library of Congress Cataloging-in-Publication Data

Fox, John, 1947–
    Multiple and generalized nonparametric regression / John Fox
    p.   cm. — (A Sage university papers series. Quantitative
applications in the social sciences ; no. 07-131)
    Includes bibliographical references and index.
    ISBN 0-7619-2189-3 (pbk. : acid-free paper)
    1. Social sciences—Statistical methods. 2. Regression analysis. 3. Nonparametric
statistics.   I. Title.   II. Series: Sage
university papers series. Quantitative applications in the social
sciences; no. 07-131.
    HA31.3.F693   2000
    300′.1′519536—dc21   00-024740

This book is printed on acid-free paper.

00 01 02 03 04 10 9 8 7 6 5 4 3 2 1

Acquiring Editor:	C. Deborah Laughton
Editorial Assistant:	Eileen Carr
Production Editor:	Diana E. Axelsen
Production Assistant:	Nevair Kabakian
Typesetter:	Technical Typesetting Inc.

When citing a university paper, please use the proper form. Remember to cite the Sage University Paper series title and include paper number. One of the following formats can be adapted (depending on the style manual used):

(1) FOX, J. (2000) *Multiple and Generalized Nonparametric Regression.* Sage University Papers Series on Quantitative Applications in the Social Sciences, 07-131. Thousand Oaks, CA: Sage.

OR

(2) Fox, J. (2000). *Multiple and Generalized Nonparametric Regression.* (Sage University Papers Series on Quantitative Applications in the Social Sciences, series no. 07-131). Thousand Oaks, CA: Sage.

CONTENTS

---

* Sections marked by an asterisk contain more difficult material. See page 7 for details.

SERIES EDITOR'S INTRODUCTION

The volume at hand builds on the author's earlier companion volume in this series, *Nonparametric Simple Regression: Smoothing Scatterplots*. In that monograph, Professor Fox showed us how to probe the data in order to trace a bivariate relationship's form, never mind how winding its course. In this monograph, we learn to estimate and plot smooth functions when there are multiple independent variables. This multiple regression is nonparametric because it abandons the linearitity assumption, instead allowing the discovery of whatever sort of continuous curve that may exist. Put another way, nonparametric multiple regression is quite a broad classification, subsuming within it that very restricted class of relationships defined by a straight line.

Local polynomial simple regression, developed in the first monograph as a nonparametric model fitting method, is extended here through local polynomial multiple regression. Two real data examples are well worked, one on the prediction of the quantitative variable of occupational prestige from education and income, the other on the prediction of the dichotomous variable of women's labor-force participation. The common problems that can arise in such analyses are explicated. First, there is the "curse of dimensionality," meaning that the local fits of the points are ever in danger of becoming less and less local, so decreasing the quality of estimates. Second, there is the chronic problem of interpretation. Consider that no unique parameter estimate is offered up, as in ordinary least-squares (OLS) multiple regression, where there is partial slope coefficient, b, indicating the expected change in Y for a unit change in X with, say, Z held constant. Instead, what is estimated is the nonparametric regression line, which reveals that the expected value of the change in Y changes, depending on where along X its unit change occurs.

That is, what is observed is a curve or a curved surface, and perhaps a rather unusual one. The way this relationship is understood, then, is graphically and that involves skills at which Professor Fox is an unsurpassed master. The interpretative graphs presented, by way of comprehending the multivariate relations under study, are second to none in their communicative power. Partly this power comes from the vivid discussion of these visuals. For example, he says, describing Figures 2.4 and 2.5, "I can *see* [emphasis added] that prestige generally rises with education...." [Or] it is relatively easy to *see* [again emphasis added]...that our hypothetical occupation with an average income of $10,000 and an average eduation level of 12 years has fitted prestige between 50 and 60 points." These things can be seen easily on these well-done figures, which convey much despite their multivariate complexity. Graphic virtuosity is even more impressive in, for example, Figure 2.8, a coplot clearly depicting the relationships among four variables—prestige, percent women, education, and income.

The difficulties of interpretation in nonparametric multiple regression prompt the investigation of further techniques from additive regression models, projection pursuit regression, generalized nonparametric regression, or regression trees, all of which are treated in separate chapters. Interestingly, Professor Fox points out that the older technique of "automatic interaction detection" (AID) is a regression tree approach, nonparametric in that it employs a binning and averaging methodology. He further notes, wisely, that this AID-type strategy is treacherous, because of collinearity problems and its blindness to theory.

In his conclusion, the author issues a call for integrating nonparametric regression into statistical practice. Hopefully, the call will be heard. For too long, analysts have submitted their data to the linear assumption or to a somewhat less restrictive family of formulas for variable transformation to achieve linearity. But, as this monograph makes clear, these constraints are not necessary. Systematic inductive examination of the data, with these methods, can draw out relationships represented by even the most unusual curves.

—Michael S. Lewis-Beck
Series Editor

ACKNOWLEDGMENTS

I am grateful to two anonymous reviewers, to Michael Lewis-Beck, the editor of the QASS series, and to Scott Long for helpful comments on a draft of this monograph. I also profited from conversations with Bob Stine and Werner Stuetzle about some of the material in the monograph. Finally, I wish to thank Deborah Laughton, my editor at Sage, for her encouragement and support.

For Bonnie and Jesse

MULTIPLE AND GENERALIZED NONPARAMETRIC REGRESSION

JOHN FOX
McMaster University

1. INTRODUCTION

Multiple regression analysis is in two senses the central method of statistical data analysis. First, multiple regression is employed extensively in research in the social sciences and elsewhere. Second, by extension and generalization, multiple regression provides the basis for much of applied statistics.

Regression analysis concerns the conditional distribution of a response (or dependent variable) y as a function of several predictors (or independent variables), $x_1, x_2, \ldots, x_k$. When the response variable is quantitative, it is usual to focus on its average value, conditional on the predictors:

$$\mu | x_1, x_2, \ldots, x_k = f(x_1, x_2, \ldots, x_k).$$

In typical applications, regression analysis is *linear least-squares regression*, a method that makes restrictive assumptions about the structure of the data. The linear regression model is

$$\mu | x_1, x_2, \ldots, x_k = \alpha + \beta_1 x_1 + \beta_2 x_2 + \cdots + \beta_k x_k$$

or, equivalently,

$$y = \alpha + \beta_1 x_1 + \beta_2 x_2 + \cdots + \beta_k x_k + \varepsilon$$

where the error ε has a conditional expectation of zero. Additionally assuming that the errors are normally and independently distributed with common variance, $\varepsilon \sim N(0, \sigma^2)$, justifies the linear least-squares estimator.

1

Nonparametric regression analysis relaxes the assumption of linearity, typically substituting the weaker assumption that the average value of the response is a smooth function of the predictors. The object is then to estimate that function, much as the object in linear regression is to estimate the regression coefficients, α and the β's.

Generalized linear models extend linear multiple regression analysis to qualitative/categorical response variables and to response variables (such as counts) that are not normally distributed. Important examples of generalized linear models include logistic regression analysis (logit models) for binary (two-category) responses and Poisson regression analysis for counts. The nonparametric regression analogs of generalized linear models similarly substitute a smooth function of the predictors for a linear function.

1.1. Two Examples

Two illustrative regression problems will be employed throughout this monograph, one for a quantitative response variable (occupational prestige), and the other for a binary response (labor-force participation).

1.1.1. Occupational Prestige

Blishen and McRoberts (1976) performed a linear least-squares regression of the prestige of 102 Canadian occupations on the average income and education levels of incumbents in these occupations. The prestige scores were derived from a sample survey in which respondents were asked to rate the prestige of the occupations; the income and education data were taken from the Canadian census. The object of this research was to use the estimated regression equation to predict the prestige levels of other occupations for which direct prestige ratings were unavailable but for which income and education data were available in the census.

The results of Blishen and McRoberts's regression are as follows, with coefficient standard errors shown in parentheses below the regression coefficients:

$$\widehat{\text{Prestige}} = \underset{(3.22)}{-6.85} + \underset{(0.22)}{1.36} \times \text{Income} + \underset{(0.35)}{4.14} \times \text{Education}$$

Here, $\overline{\text{Prestige}}$ is the predicted or fitted value of prestige. Prestige is measured in arbitrary units, which range from about 15 points (for the occupation "newsboys") to about 90 points (for "physicians"). Income is measured in thousands of dollars and education in years.

The coefficients for both income and education are several times their standard errors, and hence are highly statistically significant. The large squared multiple correlation for this regression, $R^2 = 0.798$, would be interpreted by many researchers as confirmation of the adequacy of the regression model.

1.1.2. Married Women's Labor-Force Participation

In his fine text on regression models for categorical data, Long (1997) reports a linear logistic regression of married women's labor-force participation on several predictors. This example draws on data from the 1976 U.S. Panel Study of Income Dynamics originally employed by Mroz (1987) for a slightly different purpose. The same data are used by Berndt (1991) as an exercise in linear logistic regression.

Adopting Long's notation, the response lfp is a binary variable, with 1 representing "in the labor force," and 0 representing "not in the labor force." The predictors in the logistic regression are:

Predictor	Description	Remarks
k5	Number of children ages 5 and younger	0–3, few 3's
k618	Number of children ages 6 to 18	0–8, few > 5
age	Women's age in years	30–60, single years
wc	Wife's college attendance	0/1
hc	Husband's college attendance	0/1
lwg	Log of wife's estimated wage rate	See text
inc	Family income excluding wife's income	$1000s

With the exception of lwg, these variables are self-explanatory. For women in the labor force, lwg is the log of their actual wage rate; for women not in the labor force, lwg is their log predicted wage rate. This prediction is based on a linear least-squares regression of lwg on women's characteristics for those women in the labor force. We shall see later (in Chapter 6) that the asymmetric definition of lwg for women in and out of the labor force causes difficulties.

The estimated logistic regression coefficients, along with their standard errors, are given in the following table:

Predictor	Coefficient	Standard Error
constant	3.1818	0.6420
k5	−1.4627	0.1959
k618	−0.0645	0.0678
age	−0.0629	0.0127
wc	0.8072	0.0127
hc	0.1117	0.2055
lwg	0.6046	0.1503
inc	−0.0344	0.0082

The coefficients for k5, age, wc, lwg, and inc are all highly statistically significant (with sensible signs), while those for k618 and hc are nonsignificant.

1.2. Plan of the Monograph

1.2.1. What Is Included?

- *Local polynomial regression*, a flexible method for fitting the nonparametric multiple regression model

$$\mu | x_1, x_2, \ldots, x_k = f(x_1, x_2, \ldots, x_k)$$

is the subject of Chapter 2. I develop local polynomial multiple regression as a straightforward generalization of local polynomial simple regression (which is described extensively in the companion to this monograph, Fox, 2000, Chapters 4 and 5).
- Difficulties in fitting and interpreting general nonparametric multiple regressions lead to the *additive regression model* of Chapter 3,

$$\mu | x_1, x_2, \ldots, x_k = \alpha + f_1(x_1) + f_2(x_2) + \cdots + f_k(x_2),$$

where the f_j are smooth but otherwise unspecified functions. The additive regression model is therefore more restrictive than the general nonparametric multiple regression model, in that it rules out interactions among the predictors, but it is considerably more flexible than the standard linear regression model. I also consider hybrid models that include some interactions and that include some linear terms.

- Chapter 4 describes *projection-pursuit regression*, a method that models the average response as the sum of smooth functions of linear combinations, $z_j = \alpha_{j1}x_1 + \alpha_{j2}x_2 + \cdots + \alpha_k x_{jk}$, of the predictors,

$$\mu|x_1, x_2, \ldots, x_k = \alpha + f_1(z_1) + f_2(z_2) + \cdots + f_p(z_p)$$

Projection-pursuit regression typically aims to reduce the dimensionality of the regression problem ($p < k$). Although based on linear combinations, the projection-pursuit model can capture certain kinds of interactions among the predictors.

- Chapter 5 introduces *regression trees*, which are based on successive binary divisions of the predictor space, and therefore may be viewed as extensions of binning estimators for simple nonparametric regression (see Fox, 2000, Chapter 2).

- Nonparametric analogs to generalized linear models are the subject of Chapter 6, which focuses on logistic regression for binary data. Topics considered include *local likelihood estimation* for local polynomial generalized regression models; the extension of additive regression models to binary and other non-normal data (*generalized additive models*), and the extension of regression trees to categorical responses (*classification trees*).

- Finally, in Chapter 7, I argue for integrating nonparametric regression in the general practice of statistical data analysis.

1.2.2. What Is Missing?

The statistical literature on nonparametric regression is large and growing. This monograph and its companion (Fox, 2000) are meant to provide a broad introduction to nonparametric regression analysis, but the coverage is not encyclopedic. I have endeavored to include the methods that are most used and most useful, I have often ignored small variations on specific methods, and I have emphasized techniques that are relatively easy to understand.

In particular, the following methods of nonparametric regression analysis are not covered in these monographs:

- Except for brief treatment in Fox (2000, Section 4.6), I have not described methods for special data structures such as time-series data or spatially distributed data. See, for example, Fan and Gijbels (1996, Chapter 6) and Bowman and Azzalini (1997, Chapter 7) on smoothing time-series data, and Venables and Ripley (1997, Chapter 16) for an overview of spatial smoothing.

- I have also ignored *response-transformation models*, which generalize the additive regression model of Chapter 3 by allowing for nonparametric transformation of y along with the x's,

$$f(y) = \alpha + f_1(x_1) + f_2(x_2) + \cdots + f_k(x_k) + \varepsilon,$$

where f and the f_j are smooth functions to be estimated from the data. Two methods that implement this model are Brieman and Friedman's (1985) ACE and Tibshirani's (1988) AVAS.

  — Named for its computational procedure—*alternating conditional expectations*—the object of ACE is to transform y and the x's to maximize the multiple correlation. Any of the transformations can be constrained to be monotone (order-preserving), a strategy that makes particular sense for the response transformation f, because nonmonotone transformation of y makes interpretation difficult. ACE suffers from several deficiencies, however, as outlined by Hastie and Tibshirani (1990, Section 7.2): For example, because the method maximizes the multiple correlation, the optimal transformations that it locates are dependent upon the distribution of the x's. In regression analysis, we typically want to treat the distribution of the x's as given and study the conditional dependence of y on the predictors. A nice example illustrating some of the pitfalls of ACE appears in Venables and Ripley (1997, Section 11.3).

  — AVAS is an acronym for *additivity and variance stabilization*. Like ACE, AVAS employs an alternating iterative (repetitive) method to refine nonparametric transformations of y and the x's. The transformation of y, which is constrained to be monotone, is selected at each step to make the residual variance independent of the fitted values. Although AVAS appears more promising than ACE, it is, as far as I can ascertain, little used.

On balance, the issues to which transformation of y is addressed—nonconstant error variance and non-normality—are probably dealt with most effectively by nonautomatic methods.

- The methods described here and in Fox (2000) assume that the population regression function is smooth. In particular, local polynomial regression (Section 2) and smoothing splines (Fox, 2000, Chapter 6) do not do a good job of capturing discontinuities in a regression function.[1] A relatively new approach to nonparametric regression called *wavelet regression* is better suited to representing rough or discontinuous relationships.

  Wavelet decomposition is an orthogonal series method, in which the data are resolved into uncorrelated components. The data are "smoothed" (i.e., error is eliminated from the data) by retaining only the most important components. This notion is perhaps familiar from Fourier analysis, where a function is decomposed into uncorrelated sinusoidal components; in statistics, Fourier methods are particularly useful in the analysis of periodic time-series data (see, e.g., Bloomfield, 1976). Unlike Fourier analysis, however, wavelet decompositions are naturally adapted to representing rough data.

Wavelet analysis originated in the areas of signal processing and data compression, including image "de-noising" and compression. There is a strong analogy between an image and a regression surface: We can think of a two-dimensional (monochrome) picture as representing variations in image density (y) as a function of two spatial coordinates (x_1 and x_2). In a noisy image, we want to extract the signal, analogous to the true regression surface, from the noise, which is analogous to the error in regression. Because images often have sharp edges, a method that does not artificially smooth over these edges is desirable.

I would have liked to include a section on wavelet regression in this monograph, but have not done so because of the mathematical complexity of the method. Wavelet regression does not lend itself to brief, accessible exposition. Introductions to the topic may be found in Fan and Gijbels (1996, Section 2.5) and Nason and Silverman (1994, in press).

1.3. Notes on Background, Approach, and Computing

I assume that readers are familiar with linear least-squares multiple regression and with logistic regression, and that they have been exposed to the essential ideas of statistical inference. I also assume familiarity with nonparametric simple regression ("scatterplot smoothing"), which is the subject of the companion to this monograph (Fox, 2000). Although, in the interest of continuity, there is occasional overlap with Fox (2000), the redundant material (most notably in Section 2.1) is generally treated very briefly here. Where appropriate, I have made reference to material in Fox (2000).

My goal is to write a broadly accessible account of nonparametric regression, without unduly watering down the subject. To this end, I have segregated more difficult material in sections denoted by an asterisk. The asterisked material employs calculus or matrix notation, or involves a relatively intricate argument. Statistical theory, insofar as it is introduced, is treated informally and only to illuminate the rationale for and use of nonparametric regression in data analysis.

Readers who are convinced of the utility of nonparametric regression analysis will naturally (I hope) want to employ it in their work. Although methods of scatterplot smoothing are available in some form in most statistical packages, methods of nonparametric multiple regression and of generalized nonparametric regression are largely absent. For example, at the time of writing, neither SAS nor SPSS contains procedures for local polynomial multiple regression or for generalized nonparametric regression models, although SPSS is capable of fitting regression and classification trees.

An exception is the S statistical computing environment (described, e.g., in Venables and Ripley, 1997), which is particularly strong in its nonparametric regression capabilities. S is distributed commercially as S-Plus; a work-alike called R, which includes most of the nonparametric regression capabilities of S-Plus, is available as freeware.

Another, if less widely used, exception is the xPloRe system, one of whose authors, Wolfgang Härdle, has made important contributions to nonparametric regression (e.g., Härdle, 1990).

Further information on computing, along with the datasets employed in this monograph and internet links, may be found on my web site, a link to which is provided at the Sage web site ⟨http://www.sagepub.com⟩; search for "John Fox." I will endeavour to keep the information on my web site up to date.

2. LOCAL POLYNOMIAL MULTIPLE REGRESSION

Unlike some methods of nonparametric regression (such as the smoothing splines described in Fox, 2000, Chapter 6), local polynomial regression extends straightforwardly from simple to multiple regression. The method has an intuitively appealing rationale, and it is relatively simple to implement. Moreover, local polynomial regression generalizes easily to binary and other non-normal data (as discussed in Section 6). Finally, an implementation of local polynomial regression called *lowess* or *loess*[2] is the most commonly available method of nonparametric regression.

2.1. Review of Local Polynomial Simple Regression

I assume familiarity with local polynomial simple regression and include the topic briefly here for continuity. It will help, in particular, to fix notation and terminology, and to have a convenient point of reference for basic results. A much more extensive treatment is available in the companion to this monograph, Fox (2000, Chapters 4 and 5).

The immediate aim of local polynomial simple regression is to estimate the regression function $\mu|x$ at a focal predictor value $x = x_0$. We accomplish this aim by a weighted least-squares (WLS) regression of y on x, emphasizing observations whose x-values are close to the focal x_0:

1. We need a *kernel function* $K(x - x_0)$ that attaches greatest weight to observations that are close to the focal x_0 and then falls off symmetrically and smoothly as $|x - x_0|$ grows. Given these characteristics, the specific choice of the kernel function is not critical; I shall use the *tricube* kernel. Let $z_i = (x_i - x_0)/h$, the scaled distance between the predictor value for the ith observation and the focal value. The tricube kernel function is

$$K_T(z) = \begin{cases} (1 - |z|^3)^3 & \text{for } |z| < 1 \\ 0 & \text{for } |z| \geq 1 \end{cases}$$

Thus, observations more distant than h from the focal value receive 0 weight and are effectively excluded from the local regression. The value h is called the *half-window width* or *bandwidth* of the local regression smoother. The bandwidth may either be fixed or adjusted to include a fixed proportion of nearest neighbors of the focal value; in the latter event, the proportion s of included observations is termed the *span* of the smoother. The number of observations included in the local fit is $m = [ns]$, where the square brackets denote rounding to the nearest integer.

2. Using the kernel weights, we perform a pth order polynomial WLS regression of y on x, fitting the equation

$$y_i = a + b_1(x_i - x_0) + b_2(x_i - x_0)^2 + \cdots + b_p(x_i - x_0)^p + e_i$$

to minimize the weighted residual sum of squares, $\sum_{i=1}^{n} w_i^2 e_i^2$. The fitted value at the focal x_0 is $\widehat{y}|x_0 = a$.

3. This procedure is repeated at a sufficiently large collection of focal predictor values to draw the fitted regression function; usually we use the observations x_i as the focal values.

Figure 2.1 illustrates local polynomial simple regression using the relationship between prestige and income in the Canadian occupational prestige data. Panels (a)–(c) of this figure show the calculation

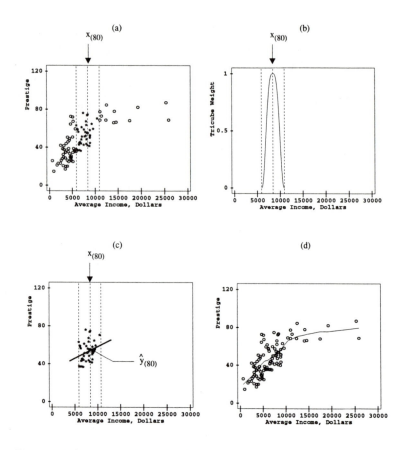

Figure 2.1. Nearest-neighbor local linear regression of prestige on income. The window in (a) includes the $m = 40$ nearest neighbors of the focal value $x_{(80)}$. The tricube weights for this window are shown in (b) and the locally weighted least-squares line in (c), producing the fitted value $\hat{y}_{(80)}$. Fitted values for all of the observations are connected in (d) to produce the nonparametric regression line.

of the fitted value of prestige, $\hat{y}_{(80)}$, at the 80th ordered value of income, $x_{(80)}$. Panel (d) shows the estimated regression curve $\hat{y} = \hat{f}(x)$ produced by connecting all $n = 102$ fitted values. Nearest-neighbor bandwidths are employed, with a span of $s = 0.4$. Thus, $m = [102 \times 0.4] = 40$ observations are included in each local fit. In this example, the order of the local polynomial regression is $p = 1$, so the local fits are linear.

2.1.1. Selecting Order and Span

The key issues in local polynomial regression are (1) selecting the order p of the local polynomials and (2) selecting the bandwidth h of the fixed-bandwidth smoother or the span s of the nearest-neighbor smoother. The general statistical goal of these choices is to minimize the mean-square error (MSE) of the estimator, which at focal value x_0 is

$$\text{MSE}(\widehat{y}|x_0) = E\left[(\widehat{y}|x_0 - \mu|x_0)^2\right]$$
$$= V(\widehat{y}|x_0) + \text{bias}^2(\widehat{y}|x_0),$$

that is, the sum of sampling variance and squared bias.

- *Order*: There is a theoretical advantage of odd order local polynomials: The polynomial of odd order $p + 1$ has the same asymptotic variance as the polynomial of even order p, but lower bias. Thus, a local cubic polynomial estimator ($p = 3$) is preferred to a local quadratic ($p = 2$), and a local linear estimator ($p = 1$) to a local constant ($p = 0$). Usually the local linear estimator suffices.
- *Span*: The bandwidth or span of the estimator can be selected by visual trial and error, by cross-validation, or by formal minimization of an estimate of the MSE.

  — In visual trial and error, we choose the smallest value of h or s that produces a reasonably smooth regression curve. It sometimes helps to examine (and smooth) the residuals from the fit, $e_i = y_i - \widehat{y}_i$, selecting the largest span for the original fit that produces residuals that are unrelated to x.
  — In cross-validation, we estimate each fitted value based on a non-parametric regression that omits the corresponding observation. We then choose the span that minimizes the cross-validation function,

$$\text{CV}(s) = \frac{\sum_{i=1}^{n}\left[\widehat{y}_{-i}(s) - y_i\right]^2}{n},$$

where $\widehat{y}_{-i}(s) = \widehat{y}|x_i$ is the fitted value at the omitted ith observation for span s.

2.1.2. Making Local Polynomial Estimates Resistant to Outliers

Local polynomial estimates are computed by weighted least-squares regression and consequently can be unduly affected by outlying data values. Taking a cue from M-estimation for linear regression (see, e.g., Fox, 1997, Section 14.3), outliers can be discounted by iterative down-weighting:

1. Fit an initial local polynomial regression, obtaining estimates $\widehat{y}_i$ and residuals $e_i = y_i - \widehat{y}_i$. Large residuals are indicative of observations that are relatively remote from the regression curve.

2. Define weights $W_i = W(e_i)$, where the symmetric function $W(\cdot)$ assigns maximum weight to residuals of 0 and decreasing weight as the absolute residuals grow. The *bisquare* or *biweight* function fits this bill:

$$W_i = W_B(e_i) = \begin{cases} \left[1 - \left(\dfrac{e_i}{cS} \right)^2 \right]^2 & \text{for } |e_i| < cS \\ 0 & \text{for } |e_i| \geq cS \end{cases}$$

where S is the *median absolute residual* and c is a *tuning constant*, balancing resistance to outliers against efficiency in the event of normal errors. Selecting $c = 7$ yields about 95% efficiency compared with least-squares regression when the errors are normal; the slightly smaller value $c = 6$ is usually used.

2.1.3. Statistical Inference

The fitted values $\widehat{y}_i$ in local polynomial regression are weighted sums of the observed y values:

$$\widehat{y}_i = \sum_{j=1}^{n} s_{ij} y_j.$$

The Smoother Matrix and Degrees of Freedom*. Collect the weights into the $n \times n$ smoother matrix $\mathbf{S}$,

$$\widehat{\mathbf{y}}_{(n \times 1)} = \mathbf{S} \mathbf{y}_{(n \times 1)},$$

where $\widehat{\mathbf{y}} = [\widehat{y}_1, \widehat{y}_2, \ldots, \widehat{y}_n]'$ is the column vector of fitted values and $\mathbf{y} = [y_1, y_2, \ldots, y_n]'$ is the column vector of observed response values. The smoother matrix $\mathbf{S}$ plays a role similar to that of the hat matrix $\mathbf{H}$ in linear least-squares regression (see, e.g., Fox, 1991).

Degrees of freedom for the nonparametric regression model may be defined in several (nonequivalent) ways by analogy to linear least-squares regression:

- $df_{\text{mod}} = \text{trace}(\mathbf{S})$
- $df_{\text{mod}} = \text{trace}(\mathbf{SS'})$
- $df_{\text{mod}} = \text{trace}(2\mathbf{S} - \mathbf{SS'})$

Residual degrees of freedom then follow as $df_{\text{res}} = n - df_{\text{mod}}$, and the estimated error variance is $S^2 = \widehat{\sigma}^2 = \sum e_i^2 / df_{\text{res}}$.

Confidence Envelope for the Regression Curve. The estimated variance of the fitted value $\widehat{y}_i$ at $x = x_i$ is

$$\widehat{V}(\widehat{y}_i) = S^2 \sum_{j=1}^{n} s_{ij}^2.$$

An approximate 95% confidence interval for the population regression $\mu | x_i$ is

$$\widehat{y}_i \pm 2\sqrt{\widehat{V}(\widehat{y}_i)}$$

Putting the confidence intervals together for $x = x_1, x_2, \ldots, x_n$ produces a *pointwise 95% confidence band* or *confidence envelope* for the regression function.

Hypothesis Tests. As in linear least-squares regression, F tests of hypotheses can be formulated by comparing the residual sums of squares for alternative, nested models. To say that two models are nested means that one model (the more specific model) is a special case of the other (the more general model). In nonparametric regression, these incremental F tests are approximate.

For example, a test of nonlinearity may be constructed by contrasting the nonparametric regression model with the two-parameter linear simple regression model, $y_i = \alpha + \beta x_i + \varepsilon_i$. The models are properly nested because a linear relationship is a special case of a general, potentially nonlinear, relationship. Denoting the residual sum of squares from the linear model as RSS_0 and the residual sum of squares from the more general nonparametric regression model as RSS_1, we have

$$F = \frac{(\text{RSS}_0 - \text{RSS}_1)/(df_{\text{mod}} - 2)}{\text{RSS}_1/df_{\text{res}}}$$

with $df_{\text{mod}} - 2$ and $df_{\text{res}} = n - df_{\text{mod}}$ degrees of freedom. This test is constructed according to the rule that the most general model—here the nonparametric-regression model—is employed for estimating the error variance, $S^2 = \text{RSS}_1/df_{\text{res}}$.

2.2. Kernel Weights in Multiple Regression

As a formal matter, it is simple to extend the local polynomial estimator to several predictors. To obtain a fitted value $\widehat{y}|x_0$ at the focal point $x_0 = (x_{01}, x_{02}, \ldots, x_{0k})'$ in the predictor space, we perform a weighted least-squares polynomial regression of y on the x's, emphasizing observations close to the focal point.

- A local linear fit therefore takes the following form:

$$y_i = a + b_1(x_{i1} - x_{01}) + b_2(x_{i2} - x_{02}) + \cdots + b_k(x_{ik} - x_{0k}) + e_i.$$

- For $k = 2$ predictors, a local quadratic fit takes the form

$$\begin{aligned}
y_i = {} & a + b_1(x_{i1} - x_{01}) + b_2(x_{i2} - x_{02}) \\
& + b_{11}(x_{i1} - x_{01})^2 + b_{22}(x_{i2} - x_{02})^2 \\
& + b_{12}(x_{i1} - x_{01})(x_{i2} - x_{02}) + e_i,
\end{aligned}$$

including linear, quadratic, and cross-product terms for the predictors. When there are several predictors, the number of terms in the local quadratic regression grows large. As a consequence, we shall not consider cubic or higher-order polynomials, which contain even more terms.

In either the linear or quadratic case, we find local regression coefficients by minimizing the weighted sum of squares $\sum_{i=1}^{n} w_i^2 e_i^2$ for suitably defined weights w_i. The fitted value at the focal point in the predictor space is then the regression constant, $\widehat{y}|x_0 = a$.

As illustrated in Figure 2.2, there are two straightforward ways to extend kernel weighting to local polynomial multiple regression:

1. Calculate *marginal weights* separately for each predictor, and then take the product of the marginal weights. That is, for the *j*th predictor and observation *i*, calculate the marginal kernel weight

$$w_{ij} = K\left(\frac{x_{ij} - x_{0j}}{h_j}\right),$$

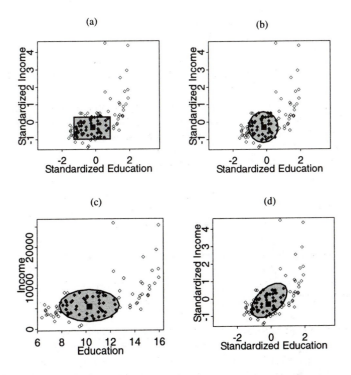

Figure 2.2. Defining neighborhoods for local polynomial multiple regression. In each case, the focal point is given by the x_1 and x_2 values for observation 83, "Radio and TV Repairmen," marked by a filled square. (a) Product marginal weights, each for span = 0.7; (b) standardized Euclidean distances, span = 0.5; (c) standardized Euclidean distances plotted on the unstandardized education and income scales; (d) generalized distances, span = 0.5.

where x_{0j} is the focal value for predictor j and h_j is the marginal bandwidth for this predictor. As in local polynomial simple regression, we can use a fixed bandwidth or we can adjust the bandwidth to include a constant number of nearest neighbors of x_j. Having found marginal weights for the k predictors, the final weight attributed to observation i in the local regression is their product:

$$w_i = w_{i1} w_{i2} \cdots w_{ik}.$$

Product marginal weights define a rectangular neighborhood around the focal x_0. Figure 2.2(a) shows such a neighborhood for the predictors income and education in the Canadian occupational prestige data.[3]

2. Measure the distance $D(x_i, x_0)$ in the predictor space between the predictor values x_i for observation i and the focal x_0. Then kernel weights can be calculated directly from these distances,

$$w_i = K\left(\frac{D(x_i, x_0)}{h}\right).$$

As before, the bandwidth h can either be fixed or adjusted to include a constant number of nearest neighbors of the focal point. There is, however, more than one way to define distances between points in the predictor space:

- *Simple Euclidean distance*:

$$D_E(x_i, x_0) = \sqrt{\sum_{j=1}^{k} (x_{ij} - x_{0j})^2}$$

Euclidean distances only make sense when the x's are measured in the same units, and even in this case, we may prefer another approach. An obvious application of Euclidean distance is to spatially distributed data, where the two predictors x_1 and x_2 represent coordinates on a map, and the regression surface traces how the average value of y changes spatially.

- *Scaled Euclidean distance*: Scaled distances adjust each x by a measure of dispersion to make values of the predictors comparable. We could use a robust measure of spread, such as the median absolute deviation from the median or the interquartile range, but the standard deviation is typically used. It is also common to center the x's by subtracting the mean from each value; centering does not, however, affect distances. The first step, then, is to standardize the x's,

$$z_{ij} = \frac{x_{ij} - \overline{x}_j}{s_j},$$

where $\bar{x}_j$ and s_j are, respectively, the mean and standard deviation of x_j. The scaled Euclidean distance between an observation $\mathbf{x}_i$ and the focal point $\mathbf{x}_0$ is

$$D_S(\mathbf{x}_i, \mathbf{x}_0) = \sqrt{\sum_{j=1}^{k}(z_{ij} - z_{0j})^2}.$$

This is the most common approach to defining distances.

For two x's, scaled Euclidean distances generate a circular neighborhood around the focal point in the standardized predictor space [see Figure 2.2(b)]. Plotted in the original, unscaled predictor space, the neighborhood is elliptical, with axes parallel to the x_1 and x_2 axes [Figure 2.2(c)].

- *Generalized distance**: Generalized distances adjust not only for the dispersion of the x's but also for their correlational structure,

$$D_G(\mathbf{x}_i, \mathbf{x}_0) = \sqrt{(\mathbf{x}_i - \mathbf{x}_0)'\mathbf{V}^{-1}(\mathbf{x}_i - \mathbf{x}_0)},$$

where $\mathbf{V}$ is the covariance matrix of the x's, perhaps estimated robustly. Figure 2.2(d) illustrates generalized distances for $k = 2$ predictors. Here, the neighborhood around the focal point is elliptical, with axes reflecting the correlation between the predictors.

As mentioned, simple Euclidean distances do not make sense unless the predictors are on the same scale. Beyond that point, the choice of product marginal weights, weights based on scaled Euclidean distances, or weights based on generalized distances usually does not make a great deal of difference.

2.3. Span Selection, Statistical Inference, and Order Selection

2.3.1. Span

Methods of span selection for local polynomial multiple regression are essentially the same as the methods for simple regression discussed in the companion to this monograph, Fox (2000, Chapters 4 and 5), and reviewed in Section 2.1; they are, briefly:

- *Visual trial and error:* We can vary the span and examine the resulting regression surface, balancing smoothness against detail. We seek the smallest span that produces a smooth regression surface.

- *Cross validation:* For a given span s, we fit the model omitting each observation in turn, obtaining a fitted value $\widehat{y}_{-i}(s) = \widehat{y}|x_i$ at the omitted observation. Then we select the span that minimizes the cross-validation function

$$CV(s) = \frac{\sum_{i=1}^{n}\left[\widehat{y}_{-i}(s) - y_i\right]^2}{n}.$$

It is, in addition, possible to derive an expression for the mean-square error of estimation in local polynomial multiple regression (see Fan and Gijbels, 1996, Section 7.8, and Simonoff, 1996, Section 5.7, for the local linear case). One could in principle proceed to estimate the MSE and to select the span that minimizes the estimate. As far as I know, this substantially more complex approach has not been implemented for multiple regression.

2.3.2. Inference

Inference for local polynomial multiple regression also closely parallels the one-predictor case. At each observation x_i, the fitted value $\widehat{y}_i = \widehat{y}|x_i$ results from a weighted least-squares regression and is therefore a linear function of the response,

$$\widehat{y}_i = \sum_{j=1}^{n} s_{ij}y_j.$$

- *Degrees of freedom**: As in local polynomial simple regression, degrees of freedom for the model come from the smoother matrix S, where

$$\widehat{y}_{(n\times1)} = S y_{(n\times1)}$$

and are variously defined as $df_{\mathrm{mod}} = \mathrm{trace}(S)$, $\mathrm{trace}(SS')$, or $\mathrm{trace}(2S - SS')$.
- *Error variance*: The error variance σ^2 can be estimated as

$$S^2 = \frac{\sum e_i^2}{df_{\mathrm{res}}},$$

where the $e_i = y_i - \widehat{y}_i$ are the residuals from the model and $df_{\mathrm{res}} = n - df_{\mathrm{mod}}$.

- *Confidence intervals*: The estimated variance of the fitted value $\widehat{y}_i$ at $\mathbf{x}_i$ is

$$\widehat{V}(\widehat{y}_i) = S^2 \sum_{j=1}^{n} s_{ij}^2.$$

Then, an approximate 95% confidence interval for the population regression surface above $\mathbf{x}_i$ is

$$\widehat{y}_i \pm 2\sqrt{\widehat{V}(\widehat{y}_i)}.$$

- *Hypothesis tests*: Incremental F tests can be formulated by fitting alternative models to the data and comparing residual sums of squares and degrees of freedom. For example, to test for the effect of a particular predictor x_j, we can omit the predictor from the model, taking care to adjust the span to reflect the reduced dimensionality of the regression problem (see Sections 2.4 and 2.5). Let RSS_1 represent the residual sum of squares for the full model, which has df_1 degrees of freedom, and let RSS_0 represent the residual sum of squares for the model omitting the jth predictor, which has df_0 degrees of freedom. Then, under the null hypothesis that y has no partial relationship to x_j,

$$F = \frac{(RSS_0 - RSS_1)/(df_1 - df_0)}{RSS_1/df_{res}}$$

follows an F distribution with $df_1 - df_0$ and $df_{res} = n - df_1$ degrees of freedom. In general, we use the most complete model fit to the data for the error-variance estimate in the denominator of the incremental F statistic.

2.3.3. Order

As explained previously, because of proliferation of terms, it is typical to consider only local linear (order 1) and quadratic (order 2) regressions. A local quadratic fit is indicated if the curvature of the regression surface changes too quickly to be captured adequately by the local linear estimator. To a certain extent, however, the order of the local regressions can be traded off against their span, because a local linear regression can be made more flexible by reducing the span. To decide between the local linear and quadratic fits, we can compare them visually or we can perform an incremental F test of the hypothesis that the additional terms in the local quadratic model are necessary.

2.4. Obstacles to Nonparametric Multiple Regression

Although, as a formal matter, it is therefore simple to extend local polynomial estimation to multiple regression, there are two flies in the ointment:

1. *The "curse of dimensionality"*: As the number of predictors increases, the number of points in the local neighborhood of a focal point tends to decline rapidly. To include a fixed number of observations in the local fits therefore requires making neighborhoods less and less local. A general assumption of local polynomial regression is that observations close in the predictor space to the focal $\mathbf{x}_0$ are informative about $f(\mathbf{x}_0)$; increasing the size of the neighborhood around the focal point therefore potentially decreases the quality of the estimate of $f(\mathbf{x}_0)$, by inflating the bias of the estimate.

   The problem is illustrated in Figure 2.3 for $k = 2$ predictors. This figure represents a "best-case" scenario, where the x's are independent and uniformly distributed. As we have seen, neighborhoods constructed by product marginal weighting correspond to rectangular (here, square) regions in the graph. Neighborhoods defined by distance from a focal point correspond to circular (more generally, if the distances are scaled, elliptical) regions in the graph. To include half the observations in a square neighborhood centered on a focal $\mathbf{x}_0$, we need to define marginal neighborhoods for each of x_1 and x_2 that include roughly $\sqrt{1/2} \simeq 0.71$ of the data; for $k = 10$ predictors, the marginal neighborhoods corresponding to a hypercube that encloses half the observations would each include about $\sqrt[10]{1/2} \simeq 0.93$ of the data. A circular neighborhood in two dimensions enclosing half the data has diameter $2\sqrt{0.5/\pi} \simeq 0.8$ along each axis; the diameter of the hypersphere enclosing half the data also grows with dimensionality, but the formula is too complicated to warrant presentation here.

2. *Difficulties of interpretation*: Because nonparametric regression does not provide an equation relating the average response to the predictors, we need to display the response surface graphically. This is no problem, of course, when there is only one x, because the scatterplot relating y to x is two-dimensional, and the regression "surface" is just a curve. When there are two x's, the scatterplot is three-dimensional, and the regression surface is two-dimensional. Here, we can represent the regression surface in an isometric or perspective plot, as a contour plot, or by slicing the surface. These strategies are illustrated in the example developed below. Although slicing can be extended to more predictors, the result becomes difficult to comprehend, particularly when the number of predictors exceeds three.

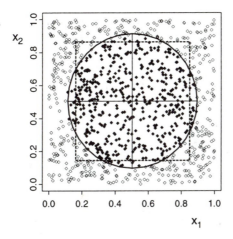

Figure 2.3. The "curse of dimensionality": 1000 observations for independent, uniformly distributed random variables x_1 and x_2. The 500 nearest neighbors of the focal point $\mathbf{x} = (0.5, 0.5)'$ are highlighted, along with the circle (of diameter $\simeq 0.8$) that encloses them. Also shown is the square centered on $\mathbf{x}$ (with sides $= \sqrt{1/2}$) enclosing about half the data.

These problems motivate the additive regression model, described in Chapter 3, and the projection-pursuit model, described in Chapter 4.

2.5. An Illustration: Occupational Prestige

To illustrate local polynomial multiple regression, let us return to the Canadian occupational prestige data, regressing prestige on the income and education levels of the occupations. Local quadratic and local linear fits to the data produce the following numbers of equivalent parameters (degrees of freedom, df_{mod}) and residual sums of squares (RSS):

Model	df_{mod}	RSS
Local linear	10.2	4,256.4
Local quadratic	17.7	4,034.8

22

The span of the local polynomial smoothers, $s = 0.5$, was selected by visual trial and error. An incremental F test for the extra terms in the quadratic fit is therefore

$$F = \frac{(4{,}256.4 - 4{,}034.8)/(17.7 - 10.2)}{4{,}034.8/(102 - 17.7)} = 0.62$$

with $17.7 - 10.2 = 7.5$ and $102 - 17.7 = 84.3$ degrees of freedom, for which $p = .75$, suggesting that little is gained from the quadratic fit.

Figures 2.4–2.7 show three graphical representations of the local linear fit:

- Figure 2.4 is a *perspective plot* (perspective projection) of the fitted regression surface. I find it relatively easy to visualize the general relationship of prestige to education and income, but hard to make precise visual judgments: I can see that prestige generally rises with education at fixed levels of income; likewise, prestige rises with income at fixed levels of education, at least until income gets relatively high. But it is difficult to discern, for example, the fitted value of prestige for an occupation at

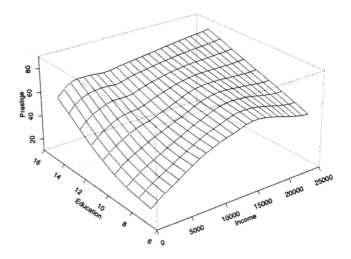

Figure 2.4. Perspective plot for the local linear regression of occupational prestige on income and education. The span of the local regression is $s = 0.5$, corresponding to marginal spans of roughly $\sqrt{0.5} \simeq 0.7$.

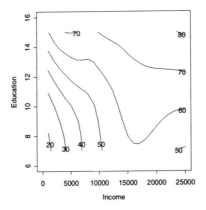

Figure 2.5. Contour plot for the local linear regression of occupational prestige on income and education.

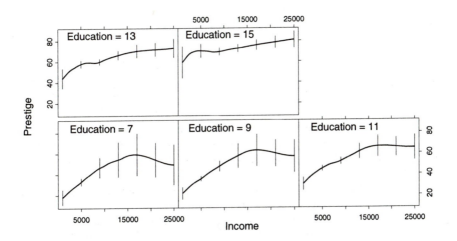

Figure 2.6. Conditioning plot showing the relationship between occupational prestige and income for various levels of education. The vertical lines give 95% confidence intervals at the indicated points.

23

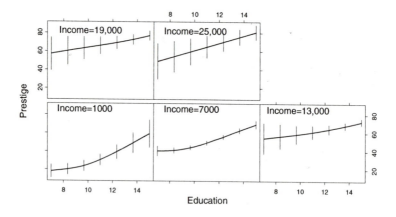

Figure 2.7. Conditioning plot showing the relationship between occupational prestige and education for various levels of income.

an income level of $10,000 and an education level of 12 years. Perspective plots are even more effective when they can be dynamically rotated on a computer, allowing us to view the regression surface from different angles, and conveying a greater sense of depth.

- Figure 2.5 is a contour plot of the data, showing "iso-prestige" lines for combinations of values of income and education. I find it difficult to visualize the regression surface from a contour plot (perhaps hikers and mountain climbers do better), but it is relatively easy to see, for example, that our hypothetical occupation with an average income of $10,000 and an average education level of 12 years has fitted prestige between 50 and 60 points.

- Figure 2.6 is a conditioning plot or "coplot" (Cleveland, 1993, Chapter 4; Jacoby, 1998, Chapter 6), showing the fitted relationship between occupational prestige and income for several levels of education. The levels at which education is "held constant" are given in each panel of the figure, which shows the fit at a particular level of education. These are the lines on the regression surface in the direction of income (fixing education) in Figure 2.4, but displayed two-dimensionally. The vertical lines in Figure 2.6 give pointwise 95% confidence intervals for the fit. The confidence intervals are wide where data are sparse—for example, for occupations at very low levels of education but high levels of income. Figure 2.7 shows a similar coplot displaying the fitted relationship between prestige and education controlling for income. It is useful to display both coplots because both partial relationships are of interest.

Is prestige significantly related to both income and education? We can answer this question by dropping each predictor in turn and noting the increase in the residual sum of squares. Because the span for the local linear multiple-regression fit is $s = 0.5$, the corresponding simple regression models use spans of $s = \sqrt{0.5} \simeq 0.7$:[4]

Model	df_{mod}	RSS
Income and Education	10.2	4,256.4
Income (alone)	4.5	11,981.8
Education (alone)	3.4	7,626.9

F tests for income and education are as follows:

$$F_{\text{Income|Education}} = \frac{(7,626.9 - 4,256.4)/(10.2 - 3.4)}{4,256.4/(102 - 10.2)} = 10.69,$$

$$F_{\text{Education|Income}} = \frac{(11,981.8 - 4,256.4)/(10.2 - 4.5)}{4,256.4/(102 - 10.2)} = 29.23.$$

$F_{\text{Income|Education}}$, for example, is to be read as the incremental F statistic for income "after" education. These F statistics have, respectively, 6.8 and 91.8 degrees of freedom, and 5.7 and 91.8 degrees of freedom. Both p values are close to 0, supporting the partial relationship of prestige to both income and education.

Perspective plots and contour plots cannot easily be generalized to more than two predictors: Although three-dimensional contour plots can be constructed, they are very difficult to understand, in my opinion, and higher-dimensional contour plots are out of the question. One can construct two-dimensional perspective or contour plots at fixed combinations of values of other predictors, but the resulting displays are confusing.

Coplots can be constructed for three predictors by arranging combinations of values of two of the predictors in a rectangular array. An example appears in Figure 2.8, extending the regression of occupational prestige on income and education by including a third predictor, the percentage of occupational incumbents who are women. The graph shows the fitted surface for a locally linear regression with span $s = 0.5$; the vertical lines give pointwise 95% confidence intervals around the fit.

- Representative levels of education, defining the rows of the display, appear in the panel at the right.

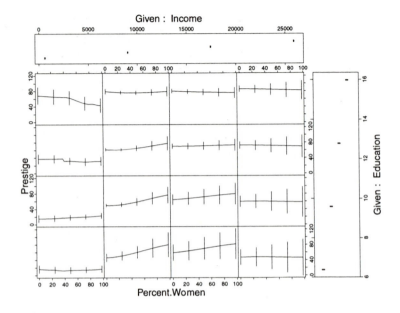

Figure 2.8. Coplot showing the relationship between prestige (vertical axis) and percent women (horizontal axis) for combinations of values of education (rows) and income (columns). Vertical lines give pointwise 95% confidence intervals around the fitted surface for a locally linear regression with span $s = 0.5$.

- Levels of income, defining the columns, appear in the panel at the top.
- Each plot in the body of the display shows the partial relationship between prestige (the vertical axis) and percent women (the horizontal axis) for a specific combination of values of education and income.

A complete set of coplots rotates the role of the third predictor: There is, therefore, another such plot for the relationship of prestige to income, controlling for education and percent women, and a third plot for the relationship of prestige to education, controlling for income and percent women. These additional coplots are not shown.

Coplots can in principle be extended to any number of predictors, but the resulting proliferation of graphs quickly gets unwieldy.

3. ADDITIVE REGRESSION MODELS

In unrestricted nonparametric multiple regression, we model the conditional average value of y as a general, smooth function of several x's,

$$E(y|x_1, x_2, \ldots, x_k) = f(x_1, x_2, \ldots, x_k).$$

In linear regression analysis, in contrast, the average value of the response variable is modeled as a linear function of the predictors,

$$E(y|x_1, x_2, \ldots, x_k) = \alpha + \beta_1 x_1 + \beta_2 x_2 + \cdots + \beta_k x_k.$$

Like the linear model, the *additive regression model* specifies that the average value of y is the sum of separate terms for each predictor, but these terms are merely assumed to be smooth functions of the x's:

$$E(y|x_1, x_2, \ldots, x_k) = \alpha + f_1(x_1) + f_2(x_2) + \cdots + f_k(x_k).$$

Because it excludes interactions among the x's, the additive regression model is more restrictive than the general nonparametric regression model, but more flexible than the standard linear regression model.

A substantial advantage of the additive regression model is that it reduces to a series of two-dimensional partial regression problems. This is true both in the computational sense and, even more importantly, with respect to interpretation:

- Because each partial regression problem is two-dimensional, we can estimate the partial relationship between y and x_j by using a suitable scatterplot smoother, such as local polynomial regression. We need somehow to remove the effects of the other predictors, however—we cannot simply smooth the scatterplot of y on x_j ignoring the other x's. Details are given in Section 3.2.1.
- A two-dimensional plot suffices to examine the estimated partial regression function $\widehat{f}_j$ relating y to x_j holding the other x's constant. Interpretation of additive regression models is therefore relatively simple—assuming that the additive model adequately captures the dependence of y on the x's.

Figure 3.1 shows the estimated partial regression functions for the additive regression of occupational prestige on income and education. Each partial regression function was fit by a nearest-neighbor local linear smoother, using span $s = 0.7$. The points in each graph

28

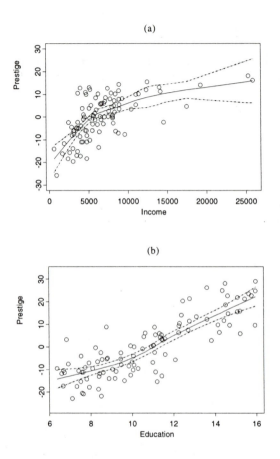

Figure 3.1. Plots of the estimated partial regression functions for the additive regression of occupational prestige on income and education. Each partial regresson uses a local-linear smoother with span $s = 0.7$. The points in the graphs represent partial residuals for each predictor. The broken lines give pointwise 95% confidence envelopes for the partial fits.

are *partial residuals* for the corresponding predictor, removing the effect of the other predictor. The broken lines mark off pointwise 95% confidence envelopes for the partial fits.

Partial residual plots are a standard diagnostic for nonlinearity in regression (see, e.g., Fox, 1991, Chapter 7; or the companion to the current monograph, Fox, 2000, Chapter 6).

- Starting with a preliminary linear least-squares regression,

$$y_i = a + b_1 x_{i1} + b_2 x_{i2} + \cdots + b_k x_{ik} + e_i$$

we form the *partial residuals* for the first predictor x_1 by adding the least-squares residuals to the linear component of the relationship between y and x_1,

$$e_{i[1]} = e_i + b_1 x_{i1}$$
$$= y_i - a - b_2 x_{i2} - \cdots - b_k x_{ik}$$

- The essential idea here is that an unmodeled nonlinear component of the relationship between y and x_1 often will appear in the least-squares residuals, so that plotting and smoothing $e_{[1]}$ against x_1 may reveal the partial relationship between y and x_1.
- The additive model extends the notion of partial residuals by subtracting the potentially nonlinear fits for the other predictors,

$$e_{i[1]} = y_i - a - f_2(x_{i2}) - \cdots - f_k(x_{ik})$$

and smoothing $e_{[1]}$ against x_1 to estimate f_1. (See Sections 3.1 and 3.2.)

Figure 3.2 is a three-dimensional perspective plot of the fitted additive regression surface relating prestige to income and education. Slices of this surface in the direction of income (i.e., holding education constant at various values) are all parallel; likewise slices in the direction of education (holding income constant) are parallel: This is the essence of the additive model, ruling out interaction between the predictors. Because all of the slices are parallel, we need only view one of them edge-on, as in Figure 3.1. Compare the additive regression surface with the fit of the unrestricted nonparametric regression model in Figure 2.4.

Is anything lost in moving from the general nonparametric-regression model to the more restrictive additive model? Residual sums of squares and equivalent numbers of parameters (degrees of freedom) for the two models are as follows:

Model	df_{mod}	RSS
General	10.2	4,256.4
Additive	6.9	4,658.2

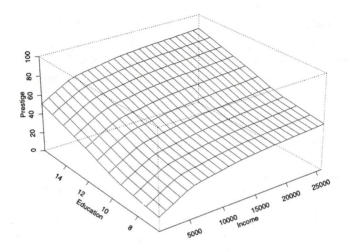

Figure 3.2. Perspective plot of the fitted additive regression of prestige on income and education.

An approximate F-test comparing the two models is

$$F = \frac{(4{,}658.2 - 4{,}256.4)/(10.2 - 6.9)}{4{,}256.4/(102 - 10.2)} = 2.63$$

with 3.3 and 91.8 degrees of freedom, for which $p = .050$—that is, just significant at the 5% level. There is, therefore, some evidence of lack of fit for the additive model.

To test the contribution of each predictor to the additive model, we compare the full additive model with models omitting each predictor in turn:

Model	df_{mod}	RSS
Additive	6.9	4,658.2
Income (alone)	4.5	11,981.8
Education (alone)	3.4	7,626.9

Then

$$F_{\text{Income|Education}} = \frac{(7{,}626.9 - 4{,}658.2)/(6.9 - 3.4)}{4658.2/(102 - 6.9)} = 17.32$$

$$F_{\text{Education|Income}} = \frac{(11{,}981.8 - 4{,}658.2)/(6.9 - 4.5)}{4{,}658.2/(102 - 6.9)} = 62.30$$

with, respectively, 3.5 and 95.1 and 2.4 and 95.1 degrees of freedom; both F statistics have p values close to 0. Because there are only two predictors, the second and third models in the table are the same as we employed to test the contribution of each predictor to the general nonparametric regression model.

3.1. Fitting the Additive Regression Model

For simplicity, consider the case of two predictors, as in the regression of occupational prestige on income and education; the generalization to several predictors is immediate (and is described in Section 3.2):

$$y_i = \alpha + f_1(x_{i1}) + f_2(x_{i2}) + \varepsilon_i.$$

Suppose, unrealistically, that the partial regression function f_2 is known, but that f_1 is not. Rearranging the regression equation,

$$y_i - f_2(x_{i2}) = \alpha + f_1(x_{i1}) + \varepsilon_i.$$

So, smoothing $y_i - f_2(x_{i2})$ against x_{i1} will produce an estimate of $\alpha + f_1(x_{i1})$.

The regression constant α is a bit of a nuisance here. We could absorb α into one of the partial regression functions. Or—somewhat more gracefully—we could force the partial regression functions evaluated at the observed x_{ij}'s to sum to 0; in this case, α becomes the unconditional expectation of y, estimated by $\bar{y}$. Then we estimate f_1 by smoothing $y_i - \bar{y} - f_2(x_{i2})$ against x_{i1}. Of course, in a real application, neither f_1 nor f_2 is known.

1. Let us start, then, with preliminary estimates, denoted $\widehat{f}_1^{(0)}$ and $\widehat{f}_2^{(0)}$, based on the linear least-squares regression of y on the x's:

$$y_i - \bar{y} = b_1(x_{i1} - \bar{x}_1) + b_2(x_{i2} - \bar{x}_2) + e_i.$$

[The parenthetical superscript (0) indicates that these are "step 0" estimates in an iterative (repetitive) process of estimation.] Then

$$\widehat{f_1}^{(0)}(x_{i1}) = b_1(x_{i2} - \overline{x}_2)$$
$$\widehat{f_2}^{(0)}(x_{i2}) = b_2(x_{i2} - \overline{x}_2).$$

Expressing the variables as deviations from their means ensures that the partial regression functions sum to 0.

2. Form the partial residual

$$e_{i[1]}^{(1)} = y_i - \overline{y} - b_2(x_{i2} - \overline{x}_2)$$
$$= e_i + b_1(x_{i1} - \overline{x}_1),$$

which removes from y its linear relationship to x_2, but retains the linear relationship between y and x_1, possibly along with a nonlinear relationship in the least-squares residuals e_i. Smoothing $e_{i[1]}^{(1)}$ against x_{i1} provides a new estimate $\widehat{f_1}^{(1)}$ of f_1. [The parenthetical superscript (1) in $e_{i[1]}^{(1)}$ and $\widehat{f_1}^{(1)}$ indicates that these quantities pertain to iteration 1; the bracketed subscript [1] in $e_{i[1]}^{(1)}$ indicates that these are the partial residuals for the first predictor, x_1.]

3. Using the estimate $\widehat{f_1}^{(1)}$, form partial residuals for x_2:

$$e_{i[2]}^{(1)} = y_i - \overline{y} - \widehat{f_1}^{(1)}(x_{i1}).$$

Smoothing $e_{i[2]}^{(1)}$ against x_{i2} yields a new estimate $\widehat{f_2}^{(1)}$ of f_2.

4. The new estimate $\widehat{f_2}^{(1)}$, in turn, is used to calculate updated partial residuals $e_{i[1]}^{(2)}$ for x_1, which, when smoothed against x_{i1}, produce the updated estimate $\widehat{f_1}^{(2)}$ of f_1. This iterative process, called *backfitting*, continues until the estimated partial regression functions stabilize.

3.2. Some Statistical Details*

3.2.1. Backfitting

Backfitting implicitly solves the following set of estimating equations:

$$\begin{bmatrix} 1 & \mathbf{0}'_n & \mathbf{0}'_n & \cdots & \mathbf{0}'_n \\ \mathbf{0}_n & \mathbf{I}_n & \mathbf{S}_1 & \cdots & \mathbf{S}_1 \\ \mathbf{0}_n & \mathbf{S}_2 & \mathbf{I}_n & \cdots & \mathbf{S}_2 \\ \vdots & \vdots & \vdots & \ddots & \vdots \\ \mathbf{0}_n & \mathbf{S}_k & \mathbf{S}_k & \cdots & \mathbf{I}_n \end{bmatrix} \begin{bmatrix} a \\ \widehat{\mathbf{f}}_1 \\ \widehat{\mathbf{f}}_2 \\ \vdots \\ \widehat{\mathbf{f}}_k \end{bmatrix} = \begin{bmatrix} \frac{1}{n}\mathbf{1}'_n\mathbf{y} \\ \mathbf{S}_1\mathbf{y} \\ \mathbf{S}_2\mathbf{y} \\ \vdots \\ \mathbf{S}_k\mathbf{y} \end{bmatrix} \quad (3.1)$$

$$\mathbf{S}_{[(kn+1)\times(kn+1)]}\widehat{\mathbf{f}}_{[(kn+1)\times1]} = \mathbf{Q}_{[(kn+1)\times n]}\mathbf{y}_{(n\times1)}$$

where

- a is the estimate of the regression intercept, α.
- $\mathbf{0}_n$ is an $n \times 1$ column vector of 0's, and thus $\mathbf{0}'_n$ is a $1 \times n$ row vector of 0's.
- $\mathbf{1}_n$ is an $n \times 1$ vector of 1's.
- $\mathbf{I}_n$ is the order-n identity matrix.
- $\mathbf{S}_j$ is the smoother matrix for the jth predictor (see Section 2.1).
- $\widehat{\mathbf{f}}_j = \{\widehat{f}_j(x_{ij})\}$ is the $n \times 1$ vector of partial regression estimates for the jth predictor, evaluated at the observed predictor values, x_{ij}.

The first estimating equation simply specifies that $a = \frac{1}{n}\mathbf{1}'_n\mathbf{y} = \bar{y}$. The remaining matrix equations, composing the rows of Equation 3.1, are each of the form

$$\widehat{\mathbf{f}}_j + \mathbf{S}_j \sum_{r \neq j} \widehat{\mathbf{f}}_r = \mathbf{S}_j\mathbf{y}.$$

Solving for $\widehat{\mathbf{f}}_j$, the fitted partial regression function is the smoothed partial residual:

$$\widehat{\mathbf{f}}_j = \mathbf{S}_j \left(\mathbf{y} - \sum_{r \neq j} \widehat{\mathbf{f}}_r \right).$$

The estimating Equations 3.1 are a system of $kn + 1$ linear equations in an equal number of unknowns. As long as the composite smoother matrix $\mathbf{S}$ is nonsingular—which would normally be the case—these equations have the explicit solution

$$\widehat{\mathbf{f}} = \mathbf{S}^{-1}\mathbf{Q}\mathbf{y} = \mathbf{R}\mathbf{y} \qquad (3.2)$$

(defining $\mathbf{R} = \mathbf{S}^{-1}\mathbf{Q}$). The size of this system of equations, however, makes it impractical to solve it directly by inverting $\mathbf{S}$. Backfitting is a practical, iterative procedure for solving the estimating equations.

3.2.2. Statistical Inference

It is apparent from Equation 3.2 that the fitted partial regression functions are linear functions of the response variable. Focusing on the fit for the jth predictor, therefore,

$$V(\widehat{\mathbf{f}}_j) = \mathbf{R}_j V(\mathbf{y}) \mathbf{R}'_j = \sigma^2 \mathbf{R}_j \mathbf{R}'_j,$$

where $\mathbf{R}_j$ comprises the rows of $\mathbf{R}$ that produce $\widehat{\mathbf{f}}_j$.

To apply this result, we require an estimate of the error variance (to be addressed presently). A more immediate obstacle is that we need to compute $\mathbf{R}_j$, which is difficult to obtain directly. Notice that $\mathbf{R}_j$, which takes into account relationships among the predictors, is different from the smoother matrix $\mathbf{S}_j$, which depends only upon the jth predictor. A simple expedient, which works reasonably well if the predictors are not strongly related, is simply to use $\mathbf{S}_j$ in place of $\mathbf{R}_j$. To construct a confidence envelope for the fit, we require only the variances of the elements of $\widehat{\mathbf{f}}_j$, which, in turn depend only on the diagonal entries of $\mathbf{S}_j$, and so the burden of computation is not onerous. Hastie and Tibshirani (1990, Section 5.4.4) suggest a more sophisticated procedure to calculate the $\mathbf{R}_j$.

To estimate the error variance σ^2, we need the degrees of freedom for error. Any of the approaches described in Section 2.3 could be adapted here, substituting the matrix $\mathbf{R}$ from the solution of the estimating equations for the smoother matrix $\mathbf{S}$. For example, working from the expectation of the residual sum of squares produces

$$df_{\text{res}} = n - \text{trace}(2\mathbf{R} - \mathbf{R}\mathbf{R}').$$

Then the estimated error variance is $S^2 = \text{RSS}/df_{\text{res}}$.

Because finding $\mathbf{R}$ is computationally demanding, a simpler, if rougher, solution is to take the degrees of freedom for each predictor as $df_j = \text{trace}(2\mathbf{S}_j - \mathbf{S}_j \mathbf{S}'_j) - 1$ or even as $df_j = \text{trace}(\mathbf{S}_j) - 1$. Then define $df_{\text{res}} = n - \sum_{j=1}^{k} df_j - 1$. Note that 1 is subtracted from the degrees of freedom for each predictor because of the constraint that the partial regression function for the predictor sums to 0; and 1 is subtracted from the residual degrees of freedom to account for the constant α in the model.

F tests for the contributions of the several predictors are based on incremental sums of squares and degrees of freedom. The incremental sum of squares for predictor j is easily found:

$$SS_j = RSS_{-j} - RSS,$$

where RSS is the residual sum of squares for the full model, and RSS_{-j} is the residual sum of squares for the model deleting the jth predictor. The degrees of freedom for predictor j are then

$$df_j = \text{trace}(2\mathbf{R} - \mathbf{R}\mathbf{R}') - \text{trace}(2\mathbf{R}_{-j} - \mathbf{R}_{-j}\mathbf{R}'_{-j}),$$

where $\mathbf{R}_{-j}$ comes from the solution of the estimating equations in the absence of predictor j. Alternatively, df_j can be approximated, as above.

3.3. Semiparametric Models and Models With Interactions

This section develops two straightforward relatives of additive regression models:

1. *Semiparametric models*, which are additive regression models in which some terms enter nonparametrically while others enter linearly. These models are therefore hybrids of the general additive regression model and the linear regression model.
2. Models in which some of the predictors are permitted to interact, for example, in pairwise fashion.

It is also possible to combine these strategies, so that some terms enter linearly, others enter additively, and still others are permitted to interact.

The semiparametric regression model is written

$$y_i = \alpha + \beta_1 x_{i1} + \cdots + \beta_r x_{ir} + f_{r+1}(x_{i,r+1}) + \cdots + f_k(x_{ik}) + \varepsilon_i,$$

where the errors ε_i are, as usual, assumed to be independently and normally distributed with constant variance. The first r predictors, therefore, enter the model linearly, while the partial relationships of y to the remaining $k - r$ predictors are simply assumed to be smooth. The semiparametric model can be estimated by backfitting. In each iteration, all of the linear terms can be estimated in a single step: Form

partial residuals that remove the current estimates of the nonparametric terms, and then regress these partial residuals on $x_1, \ldots, x_r$ to
obtain updated estimates of the β's.

The semiparametric model is applicable whenever there is reason
to believe that one or more x's enter the regression linearly:

- In rare instances, there may be prior reasons for believing that this is
  the case, or examination of the data might suggest a linear relationship,
  perhaps after transforming an x (as discussed in Fox, 2000, Chapter 6).
- More commonly, if some of the x's are dummy variables—representing
  the effects of one or more categorical predictors—then it is natural to
  enter the dummy variables as linear terms. (See Section 6.2 for an example of the use of dummy variables in an additive model.)
- Finally, we can test for nonlinearity by contrasting two models, one of
  which treats a predictor nonparametrically and the other linearly. For
  example, to test for nonlinearity in the partial relationship between y
  and x_1, we contrast the additive model

$$y_i = \alpha + f_1(x_{i1}) + f_2(x_{i2}) + \cdots + f_k(x_{ik}) + \varepsilon_i$$

with the semiparametric model

$$y_i = \alpha + \beta_1 x_{i1} + f_2(x_{i2}) + \cdots + f_k(x_{ik}) + \varepsilon_i.$$

To illustrate this last procedure, let us return to the Canadian occupational prestige data, fitting three models for the regression of
prestige on income and education:

Model		df_{mod}	RSS
1	Additive	6.9	4,658.2
2	Income linear	4.4	5,675.0
3	Education linear	5.5	4,956.0

Model 1 is the additive regression model; model 2 is a semiparametric
model containing a linear term for income and a nonparametric term
for education, and model 3 is a semiparametric model with a linear
term for education and a nonparametric term for income.

Contrasting models 1 and 2 produces a test for nonlinearity in the
partial relationship of prestige to income—that is, a test of the null
hypothesis that this partial relationship is linear; contrasting models 1

and 3 produces a test for nonlinearity in the relationship of prestige to education:

$$F_{\text{Income(nonlinear)}} = \frac{(5,675.0 - 4,658.2)/(6.9 - 4.4)}{4,658.2/(102 - 6.9)} = 8.30$$

$$F_{\text{Education(nonlinear)}} = \frac{(4,956.0 - 4,658.2)/(6.9 - 5.5)}{4,658.2/(102 - 6.9)} = 4.34$$

The first of these F test statistics has 2.5 and 95.1 degrees of freedom, with $p = .0002$; the second has 1.4 and 95.1 degrees of freedom, with $p = .03$. There is, therefore, much stronger evidence of a nonlinear partial relationship between prestige and income than between prestige and education (see Figure 3.1).

While semiparametric regression models make the additive model more restrictive, incorporating interactions makes the model more flexible. For example, the following model permits interaction (non-additivity) in the partial relationship of y to x_1 and x_2:

$$y_i = \alpha + f_{12}(x_{i1}, x_{i2}) + f_3(x_{i3}) + \cdots + f_k(x_{ik}) + \varepsilon_i.$$

Once again, this model can be estimated by backfitting, employing a multiple regression smoother (such as local polynomial multiple regression) to estimate f_{12}. Contrasting this model with the more restrictive additive model produces an incremental F test for the interaction between x_1 and x_2. This strategy can, in principle, be extended to models with higher-order interactions—for example, $f_{123}(x_{i1}, x_{i2}, x_{i3})$—but the curse of dimensionality and difficulty of interpretation limit the utility of such models.

4. PROJECTION-PURSUIT REGRESSION

Additive regression fits the model

$$y_i = \alpha + f_1(x_{i1}) + f_2(x_{i2}) + \cdots + f_k(x_{ik}) + \varepsilon_i.$$

Projection-pursuit regression, proposed by Friedman and Stuetzle (1981), fits the model

$$y_i = \alpha + f_1(z_{i1}) + f_2(z_{i2}) + \cdots + f_p(z_{ip}) + \varepsilon_i,$$

where the z's are linear combinations of the x's:

$$z_{ij} = \alpha_{j1}x_{i1} + \alpha_{j2}x_{i2} + \cdots + \alpha_{jk}x_{ik}.$$

Although the projection-pursuit model is more general than the additive regression model and in particular can capture certain kinds of interactions among the x's (see the first example in Section 4.2), it is not quite as flexible as the completely unconstrained nonparametric regression model,

$$y_i = f(x_{i1}, x_{i2}, \ldots, x_{ik}) + \varepsilon_i.$$

The hope underlying the application of projection pursuit—and the origin of the name of this method—is that when the number of predictors k is large, p can be much smaller than k, substantially reducing the dimension of the regression problem. Moreover, because the model is additive in the z's, the multiple regression problem is reduced to a series of two-dimensional fits, thus negating the curse of dimensionality.

A general problem with projection-pursuit regression, however, is difficulty of interpretation: Although it is generally an easy matter to interpret the partial regression functions produced by additive regression, arbitrary linear combinations of predictors do not usually correspond to substantively meaningful variables.

Cook and his colleagues (as summarized in Cook, 1998; Cook and Weisberg, 1999, Part III) have recently suggested a visual approach to projection-pursuit regression. Promising projections of the data are selected visually using dynamic three-dimensional scatterplots, and corresponding partial regression functions are fit by local linear smoothing. These sources also discuss two- and higher-dimensional projections, and elucidate the conditions under which one-dimensional projections can adequately capture a regression surface.

4.1. Fitting the Projection-Pursuit Regression Model*

The projection-pursuit model can be fit to data by a variant of backfitting:

1. The constant in the model is estimated by the mean of the y values, $\widehat{\alpha} = \overline{y}$, and is removed from the data by forming $y_i' = y_i - \overline{y}$.

2. Select an arbitrary initial linear combination of the x's,

$$z_{i1}^{(0)} = \alpha_{11}^{(0)} x_{i1} + \alpha_{12}^{(0)} x_{i2} + \cdots + \alpha_{1k}^{(0)} x_{ik}$$

where the superscript (0) indicates that these are preliminary values. Smooth the centered response y_i' against $z_{i1}^{(0)}$ using a standard method of simple nonparametric regression, such as local polynomial fitting or smoothing splines, obtaining preliminary fitted values $\hat{y}_{i1}'^{(0)}$. The standard implementation of projection-pursuit regression uses Friedman's "supersmoother," a symmetric nearest-neighbor, local linear estimator that selects variable spans at each x value by cross-validation.[5]

    a. Form residuals from the preliminary smooth, $e_{i1}^{(0)} = y_i' - \hat{y}_{i1}'^{(0)}$, and calculate the initial residual sum of squares,

$$\text{RSS}_1^{(0)} = \sum_{i=1}^{n} \left(e_{i1}^{(0)} \right)^2.$$

    b. Using a numerical optimization method, find the values $\hat{\alpha}_{11}, \hat{\alpha}_{12}, \ldots, \hat{\alpha}_{1k}$ that minimize $\text{RSS}_1 = \sum e_{i1}^2$. Because linear combinations of the x's that are multiples of one another define the same projection, it is necessary to place an arbitrary constraint on the α_{1j}'s; a convenient constraint is $\sum_{j=1}^{k} \alpha_{1j}^2 = 1$. A similar constraint is placed on the coefficients for each projection.

3. Having estimated the first projection, take the partial residuals from step 2 (b), the e_{i1}, and smooth these against a second arbitrary initial linear combination of the x's, $z_{i2}^{(0)}$, obtaining the preliminary residual sum of squares $\text{RSS}_2^{(0)}$. The coefficients for $z_{i2}^{(0)}$ are refined by numerical optimization to minimize $\text{RSS}_2 = \sum e_{i2}^2$, producing the coefficients $\hat{\alpha}_{21}, \hat{\alpha}_{22}, \ldots, \hat{\alpha}_{2k}$.

4. Step 3 is repeated for each additional linear combination of the predictors to be extracted, in each case using the partial residuals from the previous step. Either a preset number of linear combinations is extracted, or some stopping rule is employed. In the original paper on projection-pursuit regression, Friedman and Stuetzle (1981) propose stopping when the proportional reduction in the residual sum of squares, $1 - \text{RSS}_{j+1}/\text{RSS}_j$, is less than a small amount, such as 10%.

5. Finally, the estimated projections are refined by backfitting, at each step employing current partial residuals. The backfitting iterations cease when the estimated projections stabilize.

40

4.2. Illustrations of Projection-Pursuit Regression

4.2.1. A Simple Multiplicative Model

This first, contrived example, adapted from Friedman and Stuetzle (1981), illustrates how an interaction between predictors can sometimes be represented, perhaps counter-intuitively, as a sum of nonlinear functions of linear combinations of the predictors. Consider the model

$$y = x_1 x_2 + \varepsilon, \tag{4.1}$$

where the error ε is independent of the x's with an expectation of 0, and thus $E(y) = x_1 x_2$. The regression surface is graphed in Figure 4.1 for values of the predictors x_1 and x_2 between -1 and 1.

The predictors interact because the partial relationship between y and one of the x's depends upon the value of the other x. The reader can verify that $E(y)$ can be written as

$$E(y) = \frac{1}{4}(x_1 + x_2)^2 - \frac{1}{4}(x_1 - x_2)^2. \tag{4.2}$$

Figure 4.2 shows how the regression surface in Figure 4.1 is built up as the sum of these two components. Each component is flat in

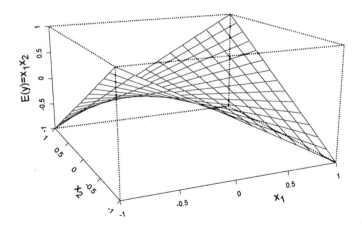

Figure 4.1. Population regression surface $E(y) = x_1 x_2$.

(a)

(b)

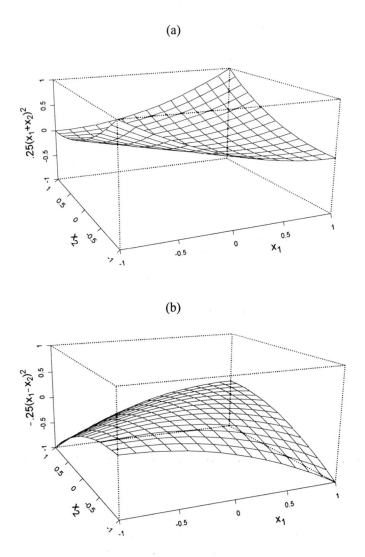

Figure 4.2. Additive components, $\frac{1}{4}(x_1 + x_2)^2$ and $-\frac{1}{4}(x_1 - x_2)^2$ of the regression surface $E(y) = x_1 x_2$ in Figure 4.1.

the direction perpendicular to the projection (i.e., for constant values of z_j).

I generated $n = 200$ observations according to the model in Equation 4.1, with x_1 and x_2 independently and uniformly distributed on the interval $[-1, 1]$, and $\varepsilon \sim N(0, 0.2^2)$. I then fit projection-pursuit regression models to the data to see if an approximation to Equation 4.2 could be recovered. Here are the R^2's for models with one, two, and three components:

Number of projections	1	2	3
R^2	.530	.722	.727

Thus, as expected, employing a second projection improves the fit, but adding a third projection does not. The linear combinations for the two-projection model are

$$z_1 = -0.774x_1 + 0.633x_2$$
$$z_2 = 0.762x_1 + 0.648x_2.$$

Taking into account the normalization of the coefficients, $\sum_{j=1}^{2} \widehat{\alpha}_{\ell j}^2 = 1$ (for $\ell = 1, 2$), these linear combinations are quite close to the components of Equation 4.2.

The estimated partial regression functions for the two projections are plotted in Figure 4.3, along with partial residuals. The quadratic character of the partial regression functions is clear in these graphs, although to my eye the span of the smoothers is too small, particularly for the first projection. Selecting the span by cross-validation often has the effect of under-smoothing the data (see Fox, 2000, Section 4.3).

4.2.2. Occupational Prestige Reprised

A general nonparametric model for the regression of prestige on income and education was fit in Section 2.5, and an additive model was fit in Chapter 3. The residual sums of squares for one- and two-component projection-pursuit models are as follows:

Number of projections	1	2
R^2	.823	.861

(a)

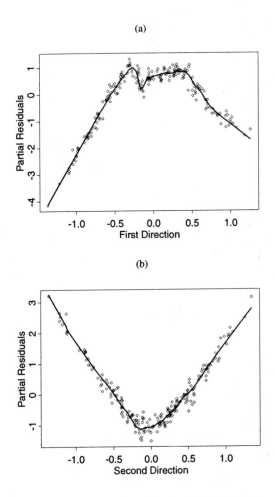

(b)

Figure 4.3. Partial regression functions (and partial residuals) estimated by projection-pursuit regression, for data generated according to the model $y = x_1 x_2 + \varepsilon$.

There is, therefore, some improvement of the fit with two projections, but in the interest of interpretability, and considering the modest size of the dataset, I shall proceed with the one-projection model.[6]

The estimated projection is

$$z = 0.00005424 \times \text{Income} + 0.9999998 \times \text{Education} \qquad (4.3)$$

At first glance, this linear combination appears to be dominated by education, but recall that the unit of income—the dollar—is very small, while the unit of education—the year—is substantial. Multiplying each coefficient by the standard deviation of the corresponding predictor, which has the effect of standardizing the predictors, produces

$$z = 2.30 \times \text{Income}^* + 2.73 \times \text{Education}^*$$

where the asterisks denote standardized variables. Because the coefficients are nearly equal, the projection is essentially the average of standardized income and standardized education.[7] Figure 4.4 shows the relationship between occupational prestige and the projection in

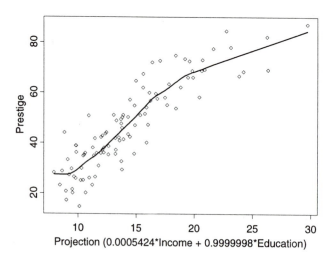

Figure 4.4. Fit of a one-component projection-pursuit model for the regression of prestige on income and education.

Equation 4.3: Prestige increases with the average of the standardized predictors, but at a decreasing rate.

It is of interest to compare the fit of the projection-pursuit model with the fit of the general nonparametric regression model (Figure 2.4) and of the additive regression model (Figure 3.2). To assist in this comparison, Figure 4.5 shows the two-dimensional fitted surface that is implied by the estimated projection-pursuit model. Although the three fits are by no means identical, they are similar for values of the predictors where most of the data fall (reflecting the correlation between education and income).

This point can be made directly by comparing the fitted values for the projection-pursuit and additive regression models, as is done in Figure 4.6. The straight line on the graph is for $\widehat{y}_{ppr} = \widehat{y}_{ar}$. Although the linear correlation between the two sets of fitted values is very high, $r = .986$, the relationship appears slightly nonlinear, with one outlier, the occupation General Managers, whose very high level of income is associated with only a modest level of education. The flattening near the bottom of the fitted values for the projection-pursuit regression is probably due to the use of symmetric neighborhoods for the local lin-

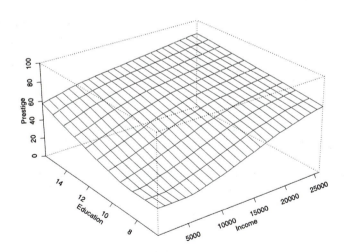

Figure 4.5. The regression surface implied by the one-component projection-pursuit regression of prestige on income and education.

46

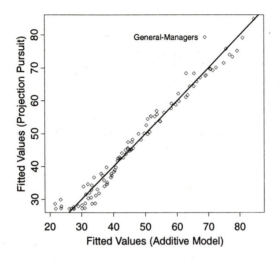

Figure 4.6. Plot of fitted values from the additive and projection-pursuit models for the regression of occupational prestige on income and education.

ear regressions; the loess smoother used to fit the additive regression does not employ symmetric neighborhoods.

Although the models are not properly nested for an incremental F test, we can assess their relative fit by comparing R^2's and degrees of freedom:

- Estimating the regression constant α consumes one degree of freedom.
- Each estimated projection uses $k - 1$ degrees of freedom, because the k coefficients for the projection have a sum of squares constrained to 1.
- Finally, the degrees of freedom used for each one-dimensional smooth can be obtained in the usual manner from the smoother matrix, e.g., as $df_j = \text{trace}(\mathbf{S}_j) - 1$; one degree of freedom is subtracted here because we have already accounted for the constant.
- Putting all this together (generalizing an argument in Venables and Ripley, 1997, Section 11.2):

$$df_{\text{mod}} = 1 + \sum_{j=1}^{p} \left[k - 1 + df_j \right]$$

$$= 1 + p(k - 1) + \sum_{j=1}^{p} df_j,$$

where, recall, p is the number of fitted projections.

The R^2's for the additive and projection-pursuit regression models fit to the occupational prestige data are very similar: .844 for the additive regression, and .823 for the projection-pursuit regression. The approximate degrees of freedom for the additive regression model (see Section 3) are $df_{mod} = 6.9$. Although the software that I employed to fit the projection-pursuit model does not report degrees of freedom (see footnote 7), I was able to approximate the fit of the model using a similar loess smoother, with span $s = 0.4$, which employs 5.3 equivalent parameters; this approximation suggests that the projection-pursuit model uses about

$$df_{mod} = 1 + 1(2 - 1) + (5.3 - 1) = 6.3$$

degrees of freedom, nearly the same as the additive regression model.

Which fit is to be preferred? Because the projection-pursuit model uses only one linear combination of the predictors and because that projection is essentially the average of standardized income and standardized education, both models have relatively simple interpretations. More generally, however, it is easier to interpret the partial-regression functions for the additive regression model, because these are in the directions of the individual predictors.

5. REGRESSION TREES

Regression trees were introduced to social scientists by Sonquist and Morgan (1964) under the name *"automatic interaction detection"* (or AID). Statistical properties of regression trees were extensively developed by Breiman et al. (1984). The specific methods to be described here are due to Clark and Pregibon (1992).

Regression trees are not always construed as methods of nonparametric regression but, as I shall explain, they represent a kind of (usually multivariate) binning and averaging. Binning estimators for simple nonparametric regression are described in the companion to this monograph, Fox (2000, Chapter 2).

Closely related to regression trees are classification trees, where the response variable is categorical rather than quantitative. Here, the original contribution was by Morgan and Messenger (1973). Classification trees are briefly taken up in Section 6.3.

An example of a regression tree for occupational prestige and one predictor (income) is shown in Figure 5.1. This kind of graphic representation of a tree is called a *dendrogram*. How the tree is constructed will be described presently; for the moment, let us focus on its interpretation.

- The *root node* of the tree, representing the entire dataset, appears (perversely) at the top of the graph. The number inside the root node ellipse is the overall mean $\bar{y}$ of prestige. The number below this ellipse is the total sum of squares of prestige, $\text{TSS} = \sum(y_i - \bar{y})^2$.
- The data are then divided into two groups on the basis of income: Occupations with average incomes less than \$7,025.50 are sorted to the left; those with incomes exceeding \$7,025.50 are sorted to the right. Now the number in each ellipse represents the mean prestige of the occupations at that node, and the number below the ellipse represents the sum of squares around the node mean.
- The observations in each node are again divided into two groups: At the left, the division takes place at income = \$3,936 and at the right at

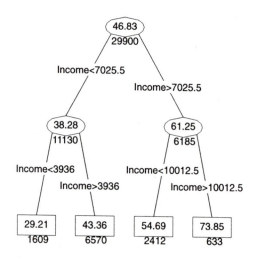

Figure 5.1. Tree for the regression of occupational prestige on income. Terminal nodes (leaves) are drawn as rectangles and interior nodes as ellipses. The number in each node is the mean of prestige for the observations at that node; the number below the node is the sum of squares around the mean.

income = \$10,012.50. The *terminal nodes* in the tree, also called *leaves*, are represented by rectangular boxes, once again containing the mean prestige of the occupations at the corresponding node. Adding up the mean-deviation sums of squares for the terminal nodes produces the residual sum of squares for the tree, RSS = 11,224.

- The terminal nodes implicitly divide the data into four irregularly spaced bins based on income: occupations with incomes less than \$3,936; those with incomes between \$3,936 and \$7,025.50; those with incomes between \$7,025.50 and \$10,012.50; and those with incomes exceeding \$10,012.50. The fitted value $\hat{y}$ for observations in each bin is then the bin average. This fit is graphed in Figure 5.2 over a scatterplot of the data; a local linear regression fit is also shown.

An example of a regression tree for two predictors, again for the Canadian occupational prestige data, appears in Figure 5.3. As in the previous example, the tree is constructed by successive binary division of the data. Each split is determined by the values of one of the predictors, education or income. The final division of the data into eight terminal nodes represents an irregular rectangular bivariate binning of the predictor space, illustrated in Figure 5.4; as in the case of a single predictor, the fitted value at each node (i.e., in each bin) is the node mean prestige.

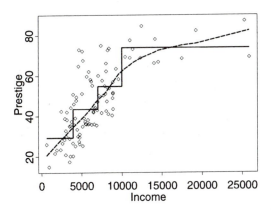

Figure 5.2. The solid line gives the estimated regression function relating occupational prestige to income implied by the tree in Figure 5.1; the broken line is for a local linear regression.

50

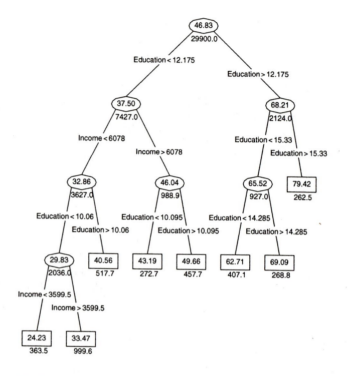

Figure 5.3. Tree for the regression of occupational prestige on income and education.

In this example, the tree is quite regular: Occupational prestige increases with education and, at least for low levels of education, with income. Compare Figure 5.4 with the contour plot for the general nonparametric regression of prestige on education and income (Figure 2.5). The difficulty of interpreting regression trees is addressed in Section 5.2.

5.1. Growing and Pruning Trees

The general idea of initially "overgrowing" a regression tree and then "pruning" it back is due to Breiman et al. (1984). As men-

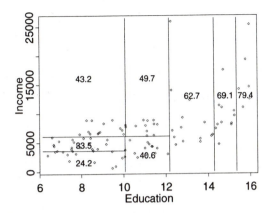

Figure 5.4. The rectangular binning of the predictor space implied by the regression tree in Figure 5.3, superimposed over a scatterplot for the predictors, income and education. The number in each bin is the mean level of prestige, which is the fitted value for the bin.

tioned, the specific approach described here is from Clark and Pregibon (1992).

Suppose that there is a single quantitative predictor with ordered values (order statistics) $x_{(1)}, x_{(2)}, \ldots, x_{(n)}$.

- Consider all binary divisions of the data that preserve order—that is, with the point of division between adjacent values $x_{(i)}$ and $x_{(i+1)}$. Then calculate the residual sum of squares that results from each of these divisions, selecting the division of the data that produces the smallest RSS. Barring tied values, $n - 1$ splits must be considered.[8]
- Similarly divide each of the two resulting nodes so as to minimize RSS.
- Repeat this procedure recursively until each terminal node (i.e., each leaf) contains fewer than 10 observations or has a mean-deviation sum of squares less then 1% of TSS. Other stopping rules are also possible, of course.

If, as is typically the case, there are several predictors, then at each stage in the tree-growing process, each predictor must be considered. For example, at the root node, we calculate the optimal binary split for each predictor and then select the predictor and split that produce the greatest reduction in the RSS.

52

Unordered categorical predictors are handled similarly, but we must at each stage consider all possible divisions of categories into two groups. For example, a predictor with categories A, B, and C produces three possible binary splits: $\{A, BC\}$, $\{AB, C\}$, and $\{B, AC\}$. More generally, if a predictor has m categories, then there are $2^{m-1} - 1$ candidate binary splits. Ordered categorical predictors are only split between adjacent categories, and thus a predictor with m ordered categories can be split in $m - 1$ ways.

These rules usually produce an overly elaborate tree. An illustration, for the Canadian occupational prestige data, appears in Figures 5.5 and 5.6. The tree in Figure 5.5 is scaled so that the vertical spacing of its nodes reflects reduction in the residual sum of squares. Figure 5.6 is scaled so that nodes are equally spaced, making it easier to see the structure of the tree and to label the nodes and branches.

Pruning balances the residual sum of squares for a tree against its complexity. Pruning a tree involves "cutting" it at a nonterminal node, literally eliminating the *subtree* growing from that node; as a consequence, the node at which the cut is made becomes a terminal node.

Define the *cost-complexity measure*

$$\text{RSS}_\alpha = \text{RSS} + \alpha \times \text{size},$$

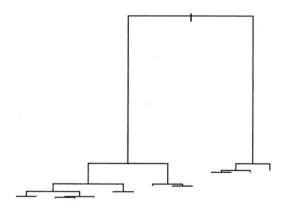

Figure 5.5. Unpruned tree for the regression of occupational prestige on income and education. The dendrogram is scaled so that the vertical separation of the nodes is proportional to the reduction of the residual sum of squares.

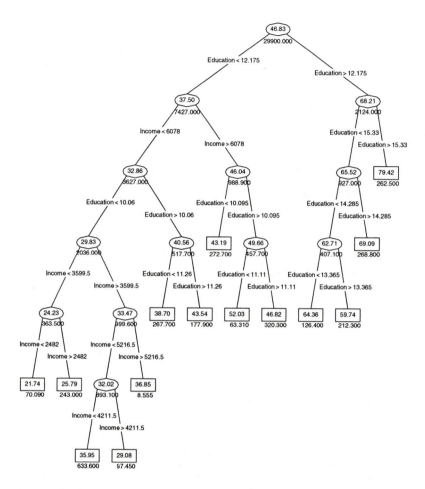

Figure 5.6. Unpruned tree for the regression of occupational prestige on income and education.

where the *size* of the tree is its number of leaves. For any given value of the parameter α we select the pruned tree that minimizes RSS_α. If $\alpha = 0$, then no pruning takes place; larger values of α produce smaller, more radically pruned trees.

How should we pick an advantageous value of α, or equivalently, an advantageous size for the pruned tree? One approach, illustrated in Figures 5.7(a) and 5.7(b), is to plot RSS against size (and α). The first of these plots is for the regression tree relating occupational prestige to income alone; the second is for the tree relating prestige to education and income. Because the tree-growing process minimizes RSS, these plots are necessarily step-wise decreasing. A relatively large drop followed by a plateau or gradual decline suggests a natural pruning point for the tree, but plots of RSS versus size are rarely so simple: There is an intrinsic problem in fitting and evaluating a tree on the same data.

We could validate the tree with new data, using the binary divisions in the tree to find fitted values for an independent dataset and pruning the tree for optimal predictions.[9] This procedure, of course, requires a second source of data, or a held-back validation subsample.

An alternative is to proceed by *cross-validation*:

1. Divide the data at random into a manageable number of parts (say 10) of roughly equal size.
2. Fit a regression tree to the data, eliminating each part in turn; thus 10 such trees would be fit.
3. In each case, obtain predicted values and the residual sum of squares for the left-out part of the data.
4. Sum the residual sums of squares over the parts of the data to calculate the cross-validated RSS.
5. Finally, plot the cross-validated RSS against the size of the optimally pruned tree (and α).

Because cross-validation randomly divides the data into parts, it may be advantageous to repeat the procedure several times, averaging over repetitions.

Examples of cross-validation plots for pruning appear in Figure 5.8(a) for the tree regressing prestige on income alone and Figure 5.8(b) for the tree regressing prestige on education and income. In the first case, the lowest cross-validated RSS is for the optimally pruned tree of size four (for which $\alpha = 357$); in the second case, the minimum RSS is for the optimally pruned tree of size eight ($\alpha = 130$). These trees were plotted in Figures 5.1 and 5.3, respectively.

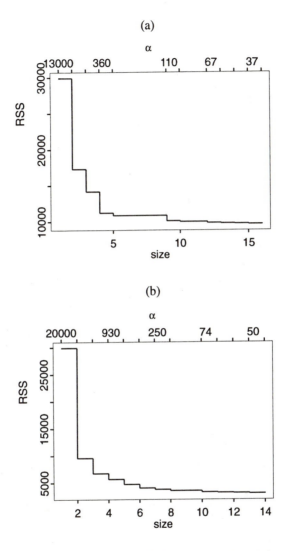

Figure 5.7. Residual sum of squares (RSS) as a function of the size of optimally pruned trees and of the corresponding cost-complexity index, α, for (a) the regression of prestige on income and (b) the regression of prestige on income and education.

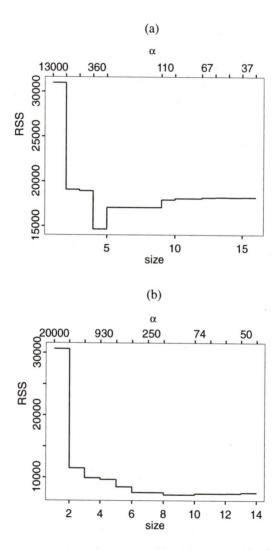

Figure 5.8. Cross-validated residual sums of squares (RSS) as a function of size of tree and the cost-complexity index, α, for (a) the regression of prestige on income and (b) the regression of prestige on income and education.

5.2. Reservations about Regression Trees

I must admit to a prejudice against regression (and classification) trees, formed when I was first exposed to these methods as a graduate student in the late 1960s. My reservations about tree-based methods pertain primarily to two issues: capitalizing on chance and difficulties of interpretation.

These issues are neither original nor new (see, e.g., Einhorn, 1972), and sophisticated advocates of regression trees, such as Brieman et al. (1984), are aware of them. In the hands of a careful data analyst armed with good diagnostic methods, regression trees can be a fruitful approach to data exploration; they should not be regarded as an automatic method of data analysis, however.

The risk of overfitting a regression tree is addressed by validating the tree on independently collected data or by cross-validation. Nevertheless, as is general in variable-selection methods (see, for example, the discussion in Fox, 1997, Section 13.2), we need to be careful not to overinterpret the results. For example, if two predictors are highly correlated, then a split on one may well preclude a split on the other, even though both splits are nearly equally effective in reducing the residual sum of squares. Likewise, although asymmetry in the tree may be indicative of interaction among the predictors, the interactions producing even dramatic asymmetry can be slight (and statistically nonsignificant).

Partly for these reasons, regression trees can be difficult to interpret—despite the fact that these methods are often touted as simple and intuitive. The data analyst should also be aware that regions of the predictor space where data are sparse tend to produce few splits, also contributing to asymmetry of the tree even in the absence of interaction. Consider, for example, Figure 5.4 for the regression tree relating prestige to education and income: There are smaller bins showing greater detail at the lower-left, where data are relatively plentiful, than at the top or to the right, where data are sparse.

Nevertheless, there are applications for which regression or classification trees seem natural, such as the identification of subpopulations particularly at risk for some phenomenon (a disease, criminal victimization, purchasing a product, etc.) or with particularly low or high values of a variable (income, for example). Trees are also useful when the object is to generate decision rules, as in empirically derived procedures for medical diagnosis.

6. GENERALIZED NONPARAMETRIC REGRESSION*

Generalized linear models (McCullagh and Nelder, 1989) encompass many of the statistical methods most commonly employed in data analysis. Beyond linear models with normally distributed errors, generalized linear models include logit and probit models for dichotomous response variables and Poisson-regression (log-linear) models for counts. Although this section does not assume familiarity with generalized linear models, I do suppose that the reader has at least been exposed to logit models (logistic regression, as described, e.g., in Aldrich and Nelson, 1984; and Menard, 1995) and to the method of maximum-likelihood (e.g., Eliason, 1993).

A generalized linear model consists of three components:

1. A *random component*, in the form of a response variable y_i, which, conditional on the predictors, follows one of the distributions in the exponential family: the normal, Poisson, binomial, gamma, or inverse-normal distributions.

2. A *linear predictor*

$$\eta_i = \alpha + \beta_1 x_{i1} + \beta_2 x_{i2} + \cdots + \beta_k x_{ik}$$

on which y_i depends.

3. A *link function* $L(\cdot)$ that transforms the expectation of the dependent variable $\mu_i = E(y_i)$ to the linear predictor η_i. Standard link functions include:

   - the identity link: $L(\mu_i) = \mu_i$;
   - the log link: $L(\mu_i) = \log_e \mu_i$;
   - the inverse link: $L(\mu_i) = 1/\mu_i$;
   - the square-root link: $L(\mu_i) = \sqrt{\mu_i}$;
   - the logit link: $L(\mu_i/n_i) = \log_e[(\mu_i/n_i)/(1 - \mu_i/n_i)]$;
   - the probit link: $L(\mu_i/n_i) = \Phi(\mu_i/n_i)$, where $\Phi(\cdot)$ is the cumulative distribution function of the standard normal distribution; and
   - the complementary log-log link: $L(\mu_i/n_i) = \log_e[-\log_e(1 - \mu_i/n_i)]$.

The logit, probit, and complementary log-log links are intended for binomial data, where y_i represents the observed number of "successes" in n_i binomial trials, μ_i is the expected number of successes, and, therefore, μ_i/n_i is the probability of success. In many applications, all of the n_i are 1, in which case y_i is either 0 or 1, and μ_i is the probability of success; this case is often described as *binary* data. The logit and probit links are very similar; in particular, both approach $\mu = 0$ and $\mu = 1$ symmetrically and asymptotically. The complementary log-log link is asymmetric and may therefore be appropriate in a generalized linear model when the logit and probit links are not. In generalized *nonparametric* regression, however, the regression curve fit to the data is flexible, and either the logit or probit link could be used to model an asymmetric approach to 0 and 1. As long as a generally reasonable link function is employed, the specific choice of link, therefore, is not crucial in nonparametric regression.

Generalized nonparametric regression models retain the random component and link function of the generalized linear model, but substitute a smooth function of the x's for the linear predictor; thus,

$$\eta_i = f(x_{i1}, x_{i2}, \ldots, x_{ik}).$$

Likewise, *generalized additive models* express the transformed expectation of y as a sum of smooth functions of several predictors:

$$\eta_i = \alpha + f_1(x_{i1}) + f_2(x_{i2}) + \cdots + f_k(x_{ik}).$$

Generalized nonparametric regression models are developed in Section 6.1 and generalized additive models (and closely related models) in Section 6.2. In both contexts, the familiar and important case of binary logistic regression will be emphasized. Section 6.3 introduces classification trees, an extension of regression trees (Chapter 5), to categorical responses.

6.1. Local Likelihood Estimation

Figure 6.1 demonstrates why generalized regression models are needed (and, incidentally, why scatterplot smoothing is particularly helpful for dichotomous responses). The figure employs Mroz's data on married women's labor-force participation, introduced in Section 1.1.

The response variable in Figure 6.1 is married women's labor-force participation, with "yes" coded as 1 and "no" as 0. The predictor is the log of the woman's estimated wage rate. Recall that the estimated

60

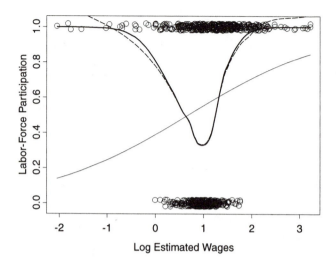

Figure 6.1. Scatterplot of labor-force participation (1 = Yes, 0 = No) by the log of estimated wages. The points are vertically jittered to decrease over-plotting. The light solid line shows the fit of a linear logistic regression; the heavy solid line shows the fit of a local linear logistic regression; the broken line shows the fit of a local linear least-squares regression. Both local regressions use nearest-neighbor windows with spans of 0.4.

wage is the actual wage rate for women who are in the labor force; for women who are not in the labor force, the wage rate is estimated on the basis of a preliminary regression of working women's wages on characteristics such as their education and age. It is clear from the graph that log estimated wages are substantially less variable for women who are not in the labor force. Although it is possible that these women are more homogeneous than those who are in the labor force, predicted values are *expected* to be less variable than observed values because the residual component of variation is missing.

The points in Figure 6.1 are "jittered" vertically (a small random component is added to the vertical coordinate) to decrease overplotting. The summary curves on the graph, however, are fit to the unjittered data. Three fits to the data are shown:

1. The lighter solid line shows the linear logistic regression of labor-force participation on log estimated wages. The relationship appears to be

positive, as expected. Fitted values between 0 and 1 are interpretable as the estimated proportion of women in the labor force at various wage levels.

2. The broken line shows the local linear least-squares fit, which suggests a very different relationship between labor-force participation and estimated wages. The fit is defective, however, in that it produces fitted values larger than 1 at the extremes of estimated wages—impossible values for a proportion. Although a kernel estimate does not suffer from this defect, it exhibits greater boundary bias.[10] Moreover, assumptions of constant error variance and normal errors are insupportable for dichotomous data. If you are familiar with logistic regression, this critique of the application of linear least squares to binary data is likely familiar as well (see, for example, Fox, 1997, Section 15.1; Long, 1997, Section 3.1.1; or Menard, 1995).

3. The heavier solid line shows a local linear logistic regression of the kind to be described in this section. The fit is similar to that of the local least-squares regression except when the fitted proportion gets close to 1. The curvilinear pattern of the regression function is probably best regarded as an artifact of the construction of estimated wages: Because estimated wages are less variable for women not in the labor force, more extreme values of this variable are observed at both ends of the wage distribution for those in the labor force. In any event, it is clear that a linear logistic regression (the lighter solid line) does not describe the data well.

Generalized linear models are typically estimated by the method of maximum likelihood. The log-likelihood for these models takes the general form

$$\log_e \mathcal{L} = \sum_{i=1}^{n} l(\mu_i; y_i)$$

where the y_i are the observed values of the response variable, and

$$\mu_i = E(y_i) = L^{-1}(\alpha + \beta_1 x_{i1} + \beta_2 x_{i2} + \cdots + \beta_k x_{ik}).$$

Here, L^{-1} is the inverse of the link function. For example, for a binary logistic regression model, the components of the log-likelihood are

$$l(\mu_i; y_i) = y_i \log_e \mu_i + (1 - y_i) \log_e (1 - \mu_i)$$

and the expected value of y is

$$\mu_i = L^{-1}(\alpha + \beta_1 x_{i1} + \beta_2 x_{i2} + \cdots + \beta_k x_{ik})$$
$$= \frac{1}{1 + \exp[-(\alpha + \beta_1 x_{i1} + \beta_2 x_{i2} + \cdots + \beta_k x_{ik})]}.$$

The maximum-likelihood estimates of the parameters are the values $\widehat{\alpha}, \widehat{\beta}_1, \ldots, \widehat{\beta}_k$ that maximize $\log_e \mathcal{L}$.

In generalized nonparametric regression, we estimate the regression function at some set of focal values of the predictors. For simplicity, suppose that there is one predictor x, that the response variable is dichotomous, and that we want to estimate $\mu | x_0$ at the focal value x_0. We can perform a logistic polynomial regression of the form

$$\log_e \frac{\mu_i}{1 - \mu_i} = \alpha + \beta_1(x_i - x_0) + \beta_2(x_i - x_0)^2 + \cdots + \beta_p(x_i - x_0)^p$$

maximizing the weighted log-likelihood

$$\log_e \mathcal{L}_w = \sum_{i=1}^{n} w_i l(\mu_i; y_i)$$

where the $w_i = K[(x_i - x_0)/h]$ are kernel weights. Then $\widehat{\mu} | x_0 = L^{-1}(\widehat{\alpha})$.

To trace the estimated regression curve, as in Figure 6.1, we repeat this procedure for representative values of x or at the observed x_i. As in local polynomial least-squares regression, the window half-width h either can be fixed or can be adjusted to include a fixed number of nearest neighbors of the focal x_0. The extension of this approach to multiple regression is straightforward, although the curse of dimensionality and the difficulty of interpreting higher-dimensional fits are no less a problem than in local least-squares regression.

6.2. Generalized Additive Models

As explained in the previous section, the generalized additive model replaces the parametric terms in the generalized linear model with smooth terms in the predictors:

$$\eta_i = \alpha + f_1(x_{i1}) + f_2(x_{i2}) + \cdots + f_k(x_{ik}).$$

Local likelihood, however, cannot be easily adapted to estimating the generalized additive model. An alternative is to adapt the method of *iteratively reweighted least squares* (IRLS), which is typically used to obtain maximum-likelihood estimates for generalized linear models.

As before, I shall focus on binary logistic regression. Results for other generalized regression models follow a similar pattern. Consider the linear logit model

$$\log_e \frac{\mu_i}{1 - \mu_i} = \alpha + \beta_1 x_{i1} + \beta_2 x_{i2} + \cdots + \beta_k x_{ik}.$$

To fit the linear logit model by IRLS, start with preliminary estimates of the parameters $(\alpha^{(0)}, \beta_1^{(0)}, \ldots, \beta_k^{(0)})$, for example, by setting

$$\alpha^{(0)} = \log_e \frac{\sum y_i}{n - \sum y_i}$$

$$\text{all } \beta_j^{(0)} = 0.$$

Then calculate the *pseudo-response variable*

$$z_i^{(0)} = \eta_i^{(0)} + \frac{y_i - \mu_i^{(0)}}{\mu_i^{(0)}\left(1 - \mu_i^{(0)}\right)}$$

and weights

$$w_i^{(0)} = \mu_i^{(0)}\left(1 - \mu_i^{(0)}\right),$$

where the preliminary estimate of the linear predictor is

$$\eta_i^{(0)} = \alpha^{(0)} + \beta_1^{(0)} x_{i1} + \beta_2^{(0)} x_{i2} + \cdots + \beta_k^{(0)} x_{ik}$$

and the preliminary estimate of the probability of response is

$$\mu_i^{(0)} = \frac{1}{1 + \exp\left(-\eta_i^{(0)}\right)}.$$

Updated estimates $\alpha^{(1)}, \beta_1^{(1)}, \ldots, \beta_k^{(1)}$ of the regression parameters are obtained by weighted least-squares regression of the pseudo-response $z_i^{(0)}$ on the x's, using the $w_i^{(0)}$ as weights. This process is iterated until the regression coefficients stabilize, producing the maximum-likelihood estimates $\hat{\alpha}, \hat{\beta}_1, \ldots, \hat{\beta}_k$.

To estimate the additive logistic regression model

$$\log_e \frac{\mu_i}{1 - \mu_i} = \alpha + f_1(x_{i1}) + f_2(x_{i2}) + \cdots + f_k(x_{ik}).$$

IRLS estimation can be combined with backfitting (introduced in Section 3.1):

1. Pick starting values of the regression constant and the partial regression functions, such as

$$\alpha^{(0)} = \log_e \frac{\sum y_i}{n - \sum y_i}$$

all $f_j^{(0)}(x_{ij}) = 0$

2. Using these initial values, calculate pseudo-response values and weights:

$$z_i^{(0)} = \eta_i^{(0)} + \frac{y_i - \mu_i^{(0)}}{\mu_i^{(0)}\left(1 - \mu_i^{(0)}\right)}$$

$$w_i^{(0)} = \mu_i^{(0)}\left(1 - \mu_i^{(0)}\right),$$

where

$$\eta_i^{(0)} = \alpha^{(0)} + f_1^{(0)}(x_{i1}) + f_2^{(0)}(x_{i2}) + \cdots + f_k^{(0)}(x_{ik})$$

$$\mu_i^{(0)} = \frac{1}{1 + \exp\left(-\eta_i^{(0)}\right)}.$$

3. Find new values $\alpha^{(1)}$ and $f_1^{(1)}, \ldots, f_k^{(1)}$ by applying the backfitting procedure to the weighted additive regression of $z^{(0)}$ on the x's, using the $w_i^{(0)}$ as weights.

4. Return to Step 2 to compute new pseudo-response values and weights based on the updated values $\alpha^{(1)}$ and $f_1^{(1)}, \ldots, f_k^{(1)}$. Repeat this procedure until the estimates stabilize, producing $\hat{\alpha}$ and $\hat{f}_1, \ldots, \hat{f}_k$.

Notice that this estimation procedure is doubly iterative, because each backfitting step (Step 3) requires iteration.

6.2.1. Statistical Inference

Once again, I shall concentrate on binary logistic regression, with similar results applying to other generalized additive models. Similar results also apply to generalized nonparametric regression models estimated by local likelihood.

After the IRLS backfitting procedure converges, the fitted values can be written as a linear transformation of the pseudo-response values,

$$\widehat{\eta}_i = r_{i1}z_1 + r_{i2}z_2 + \cdots + r_{in}z_n = \sum_{j=1}^{n} r_{ij}z_j.$$

The pseudo-response z_j has estimated asymptotic (i.e., large sample) variance $1/[\widehat{\mu}_j(1 - \widehat{\mu}_j)]$, and because the observations are asymptotically independent, the estimated asymptotic variance of $\widehat{\eta}_i$ is[11]

$$\widehat{\mathcal{V}}(\widehat{\eta}_i) = \sum_{j=1}^{n} \frac{r_{ij}^2}{\widehat{\mu}_j(1 - \widehat{\mu}_j)}.$$

An approximate pointwise 95-percent confidence band for the fitted regression surface follows as

$$\widehat{\eta}_i \pm 2\sqrt{\widehat{\mathcal{V}}(\widehat{\eta}_i)}.$$

If desired, the endpoints of the confidence band can be transformed to the probability scale by using $\mu = 1/[1 + \exp(-\eta)]$. Employing results analogous to those in Section 3.2.2, approximate confidence bands can also be constructed for the individual partial regression functions, f_j.

Likelihood ratio tests of hypotheses for generalized linear models are typically formulated in terms of the *deviance* for alternative, nested models. The deviance for a model is the log-likelihood ratio statistic contrasting the model with a maximally specified or "saturated" model, which in effect dedicates a parameter to each observation. Let $l(\boldsymbol{\mu};\mathbf{y})$ represent the log-likelihood for the model in question, and $l(\mathbf{y}; \mathbf{y})$ the log-likelihood for the saturated model. The deviance is then

$$D(\boldsymbol{\mu}; \mathbf{y}) = -2[l(\boldsymbol{\mu}; \mathbf{y}) - l(\mathbf{y}; \mathbf{y})].$$

The deviance is a generalization of the residual sum of squares for a linear model with normal errors.

For the binary linear logit model, the log-likelihood for the saturated model is 0, leading to a particularly simple expression for the deviance:

$$
\begin{aligned}
D(\boldsymbol{\mu}; \mathbf{y}) &= -2l(\boldsymbol{\mu}; \mathbf{y}) \\
&= -2 \sum_{i=1}^{n} l(\mu_i; y_i) \\
&= -2 \sum_{i=1}^{n} \left[y_i \log_e \widehat{\mu}_i + (1 - y_i) \log_e (1 - \widehat{\mu}_i) \right].
\end{aligned}
$$

The degrees of freedom associated with the deviance are n minus the number of parameters in the model. The log-likelihood ratio statistic for contrasting nested models is the difference in the deviances for the two models. This statistic follows an asymptotic chi square distribution, with degrees of freedom given by the difference in the number of parameters for the models.

Tests based on the deviance can be extended by analogy to generalized nonparametric regression models, including generalized additive models. Degrees of freedom can be defined analogously to nonparametric regression models, as described in Fox (2000, Section 5.3) and in Sections 2.1, 2.3, and 3.2 of the current monograph (also see Hastie and Tibshirani, 1990, Section 6.8.3).

6.2.2. An Illustration: Labor-Force Participation

I shall adapt an example that appears in Long (1997, Section 3.3), based on Mroz's married women's labor-force participation data (introduced in Section 1.1). I substitute a semiparametric logistic regression for the linear logistic regression in Long.

The response variable is binary: labor-force participation (lfp). The predictor variables are as follows, adopting the variable designations employed by Long (1997, Table 3.1):[12]

Predictor	Description	Remarks
k5	Number of children ages 5 and younger	0–3, few 3's
k618	Number of children ages 6 to 18	0–8, few > 5
age	Women's age in years	30–60, single years
wc	Wife's college attendance	0/1
hc	Husband's college attendance	0/1
inc	Family income excluding wife's income	$1000s

Because k5 and k618 are discrete predictors with small numbers of distinct values, I chose to model these terms as sets of dummy regressors, capable of capturing any form of partial relationship to labor-force participation. There are only three observations for which k5 exceeds 2 and only three observations for which k618 exceeds 5; I could have combined the highest categories of each of these variables, but I did not do so to facilitate tests for linearity (see below). wc and hc are also dummy regressors, representing dichotomous predictors. age and inc are modeled using nearest-neighbor locally linear logistic smoothers; in each case, visual trial and error suggested a span of 0.5.

Figure 6.2 graphs the estimated partial regression functions for the semiparametric logistic regression fit to Mroz's data (Model 1 in Table 6.1). Each panel of the figure shows the partial regression function for one of the predictors, along with a pointwise 95% confidence envelope and partial residuals. The vertical (lfp) axis of each plot is on the logit scale.

Panels (a) and (b) of Figure 6.2, for age and family income, show the fit of local partial logistic regressions. The nonlinearity in each of these partial regressions appears slight; we shall determine presently whether the departure from linearity is statistically significant. The partial regression for children 5 and under, in panel (c), also appears nearly linear, particularly discounting the fit at k5 = 3, where there are only three observations (and where, therefore, the confidence interval around the fit is very wide). Labor-force participation seems essentially unrelated to number of children 6 to 18, in panel (d); the fits at k618 = 5, 7, and 8 are each based on only one observation, and the confidence band for the fit is consequently very wide at these

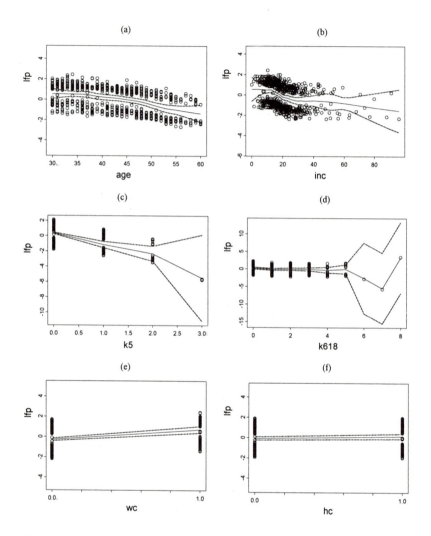

Figure 6.2. Estimated partial regression functions for the semiparametric logistic regression of married women's labor-force participation (lfp) on age, family income (inc), children 5 and under (k5), children 6 to 18 (k618), wife's college attendance (wc), and husband's college attendance (hc). The broken lines show approximate pointwise 95% confidence envelopes. The points in each panel are partial residuals for the corresponding predictor.

points. Labor-force participation appears to rise with wife's college attendance [panel (e)], and is apparently unrelated to husband's college attendance [panel (f)].

Table 6.1 shows the deviance and residual degrees of freedom for several models fit to Mroz's data, from which I calculated the following tests for nonlinearity, all of which are nonsignificant:

Predictor	Models Contrasted	Difference in Deviance	df	p
age	2 − 1	3.64	2.7	.24
inc	3 − 1	6.65	3.8	.14
k5	4 − 1	0.63	2.0	.73
k618	5 − 1	5.30	7.0	.62

An overall test, contrasting the linear logit model (0) with the semiparametric logit model (1), produces a difference in deviance of 15.62 on 15.5 degrees of freedom, which is also nonsignificant ($p = .44$).

To test for each of the terms in the semiparametric model, I fit the additional models in Table 6.2, from which I calculated the following

TABLE 6.1

Deviances and Residual Degrees of Freedom for Models Fit to Mroz's Labor-Force Participation Data

Model	Predictors						Deviance	df_{res}
	age	inc	k5	k618	wc	hc		
0	L	L	L	L	D	D	922.27	746.0
1	S	S	D	D	D	D	906.65	730.5
2	L	S	D	D	D	D	910.29	733.2
3	S	L	D	D	D	D	913.30	734.4
4	S	S	L	D	D	D	907.28	732.5
5	S	S	D	L	D	D	911.95	737.5

The following code is used for terms in the models: L, a linear term; D, a dummy regressor or set of dummy regressors; S, a local linear logit smooth.

TABLE 6.2

Deviances and Residual Degrees of Freedom for Additional Models
Fit to Mroz's Labor-Force Participation Data

Model	age	inc	k5	k618	wc	hc	Deviance	df_{res}
				Predictors				
6	—	S	D	D	D	D	935.40	734.1
7	S	—	D	D	D	D	930.34	735.4
8	S	S	—	D	D	D	968.46	733.5
9	S	S	D	—	D	D	914.14	738.5
10	S	S	D	D	—	D	927.29	731.5
11	S	S	D	D	D	—	907.76	731.5

A dash (—) indicates an omitted term.

analysis of deviance table:

Predictor	Models Contrasted	Difference in Deviance	df	p
age	6 − 1	28.75	3.6	<.00001
inc	7 − 1	23.69	4.8	.0002
k5	8 − 1	61.81	3.0	≪.00001
k618	9 − 1	7.49	8.0	.48
wc	10 − 1	20.64	1.0	<.00001
hc	11 − 1	1.11	1.0	.29

There is, therefore, strong evidence of partial relationships of women's labor-force participation to age, family income, children 5 and under, and wife's college attendance, but not to children 6 to 18 or to husband's college attendance.

In summary, the linear logistic regression model appears to summarize these data well, once the problematic estimated log wage variable is omitted.

6.3. Classification Trees

Classification trees are very much like the regression trees of Chapter 5, but for a dichotomous (two-category) or polytomous (several-category) response variable in place of the quantitative response. As a consequence, the deviance replaces the residual sums of squares as the measure of error:

- For a dichotomous response, the deviance at leaf (terminal node) ℓ of the tree is

$$D_\ell = -2[n_{1\ell} \log_e \widehat{\mu}_\ell + n_{0\ell} \log_e(1 - \widehat{\mu}_\ell)],$$

where $n_{1\ell}$ is the number of observations in leaf ℓ for which $y = 1$, $n_{0\ell}$ is the number of observations in the leaf for which $y = 0$, and $\widehat{\mu}_\ell = n_{1\ell}/(n_{0\ell} + n_{1\ell})$ is the sample proportion of 1's in the leaf.

- For a polytomous, m-category response, the deviance at leaf ℓ is

$$D_\ell = -2\sum_{j=1}^{m} n_{j\ell} \log_e \widehat{\mu}_{j\ell},$$

where $n_{j\ell}$ is the number of observations in leaf ℓ that are in category j of the response variable and $\widehat{\mu}_{j\ell}$ is the sample proportion of observations in this category.

- The deviance for the tree is the sum of deviances for its L leaves, $D = \sum_{\ell=1}^{L} D_\ell$.

- Substituting the deviance for the residual sum of squares, procedures for growing, pruning, and cross-validating classification trees are the same as those for regression trees.

An illustration, for Mroz's labor-force data, appears in Figures 6.3 and 6.4. The response here is dichotomous (labor-force participation, "yes" or "no") and the predictors are the same as those employed in the additive logistic regression in Section 6.2.2.

The unpruned tree [Figure 6.3(a)] has 100 leaves, and as is often the case, a plot of deviance against tree size [Figure 6.3(b)] is uninformative about how the tree should be pruned: There is no obvious size at which the deviance drops precipitously and then decays gradually. A drastically pruned tree, with only three leaves, appears in Figure 6.4(a). The tree was pruned by plotting the cross-validation deviance against size, as shown in Figure 6.4(b). This plot was constructed by five-fold cross-validation (i.e., based on dividing the data randomly into five parts), repeated 10 times and averaged.[13]

A classification tree provides a decision procedure for predicting the value of the response variable. The so-called "Bayes" rule takes the predicted value as the category with the largest sample proportion at the node to which an observation belongs. In Figure 6.4(a),

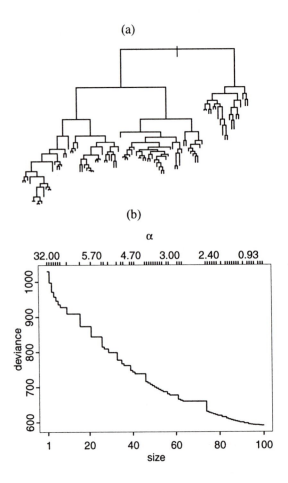

Figure 6.3. Classification tree for several predictors of married women's labor-force participation. (a) The dendrogram of the unpruned tree. (b) The deviance as a function of size of optimally pruned trees and of the cost-complexity index, α.

the Bayes-rule prediction is shown in each node of the tree, and the misclassification error rate is given below the node. For example, of the 147 women who have one or more children 5 years old or younger ("k5 > 0.5"), 53 are in the labor force ("Y") and 94 are not in the labor force ("N"). The Bayes-rule prediction is that each of these

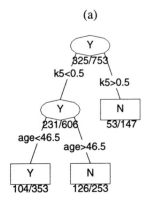

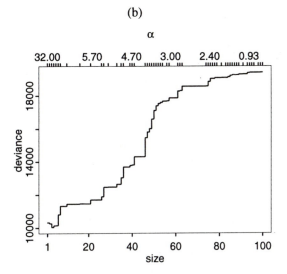

Figure 6.4. (a) Pruned classification tree for predicting married women's labor-force participation. The Bayes rule prediction is shown in each node, and the misclassification error rate (errors/number of observations) is shown below the node. (b) The cross-validation deviance as a function of size of pruned trees and of the cost-complexity index, α.

women is in the labor force (and so the corresponding node is labeled "N"), yielding an error rate of $53/147 = 0.36$.

The result is very simple: Women with one or more children age 5 or under are predicted to be out of the labor force; those with no young children are predicted to be in the labor force if they are less than 46.5 years old, or out of the labor force if they are older than 46.5. The other predictors are not used. Compare this result with the additive logistic regression model fit to Mroz's data in Section 6.2.2.

7. CONCLUDING REMARKS: INTEGRATING NONPARAMETRIC REGRESSION IN STATISTICAL PRACTICE

In the companion to this monograph, Fox (2000, Chapter 6), I argue that one of the principal applications of nonparametric simple regression is smoothing diagnostic plots. For example, smoothing partial-residual plots constructed for a preliminary linear least-squares regression may reveal nonlinear partial relationships. Nonlinear relationships detected in partial residual plots can often be accommodated by transforming a predictor or by fitting a respecified parametric model, such as a quadratic regression.

Generalized and multiple nonparametric regression can also serve in diagnostic roles. A generalized additive model, for example, can in certain instances reflect nonlinearity more accurately than the usual partial residual plots. The work of Cook and his colleagues on partial residual plots (summarized in Cook and Weisberg, 1999, Chapter 16; and Cook, 1998, Chapter 14) suggests that strong, nonlinear relationships between predictors, coupled with a strong, nonlinear relationship between a predictor and the response, can distort partial residual plots.[14]

A contrived (and extreme) example appears in Figure 7.1. The predictor x_1 in this example was generated by sampling 100 observations from the uniform distribution on the interval $[0, 1]$. The second predictor was then constructed according to the equation, $x_2 = |x_1 - 0.5| + \delta$, where $\delta \sim N(0, 0.02^2)$. The relationship between x_1 and x_2, shown in panel (a) of Figure 7.1, is strong and highly nonlinear. Finally, response values were generated as

$$y = 2(x_1 - 0.5)^2 + x_2 + \varepsilon,$$

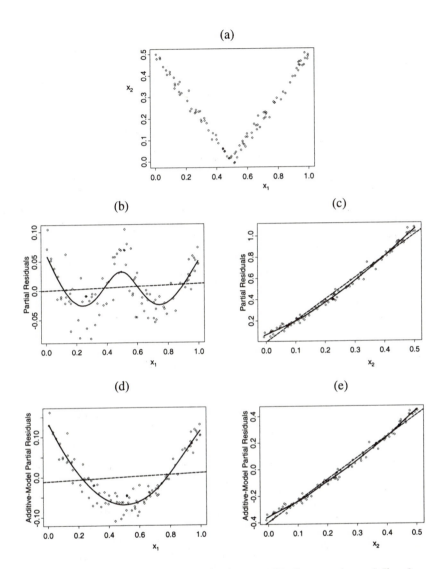

Figure 7.1. Contrived regression data: $x_1 \sim U[0, 1]$; $x_2 = |x_1 - 0.5| + \delta$, where $\delta \sim N(0, 0.02^2)$; $y = 2(x_1 - 0.5)^2 + x_2 + \varepsilon$, where $\varepsilon \sim N(0, 0.02^2)$. (a) Relationship between x_1 and x_2. (b) and (c) Partial residual plots for a linear least-squares regression; the solid line is for a smoothing spline with six equivalent parameters; the broken line is for the linear least-squares fit. (d) and (e) Partial plots for an additive regression using smoothing splines each with 6 degrees of freedom (solid lines).

where $\varepsilon \sim N(0, 0.02^2)$. The partial relationship of y to x_1 is therefore strongly nonlinear, but the partial relationship of y to x_2 is linear.

Panels (b) and (c) of Figure 7.1 show partial residual plots for a preliminary linear least-squares regression of y on x_1 and x_2. The curve on each plot is for a smoothing spline with six equivalent parameters. The linear least-squares line, representing an edge-on view of the regression plane, is also shown. Both partial relationships are substantially distorted: The relationship between y and x_1 appears to be quartic rather than quadratic; the relationship between y and x_2 appears to be slightly but systematically nonlinear. These kinds of distortions in partial residual plots are called "leakage."

Panels (d) and (e) of Figure 7.1 show the estimated partial regression functions for an additive-regression model fit to the data. The additive model also employs smoothing splines, each with 6 degrees of freedom. Similar results are obtained using locally linear smoothers. The partial plot in panel (d) clearly recovers the quadratic relationship between y and x_1; the partial plot in panel (e) still shows slight, but apparently systematic (and statistically significant), spurious nonlinearity.

Turning to real data, Figure 7.2 extends an additive regression model used as an illustration in Chapter 3 by including the percentage of occupational incumbents who are women, along with income and education, as predictors of occupational prestige. The model employs local linear least-squares smoothers, with spans of 0.6 for income and education and 0.8 for percent women. Figure 7.2 shows the estimated partial regression functions, along with pointwise 95% confidence intervals and partial residuals from the additive model. All three terms in the model are highly statistically significant, as is the nonlinear component of each partial regression.

We could accept this model as a description of the data—employing it, for example, for Blishen and McRoberts's (1976) original purpose of predicting the prestige of other occupations—or we could use the information from the additive regression to formulate a respecified parametric model for the data. The partial regression functions in Figure 7.2 for income and education are monotone (strictly increasing) and reasonably simple, suggesting that power transformations of income and education might serve to straighten their relationship to prestige. As it turns out, the log-transformation of income and the square of education appear to work well.[15] The U-shaped pattern of the partial regression function for percent women suggests fitting a

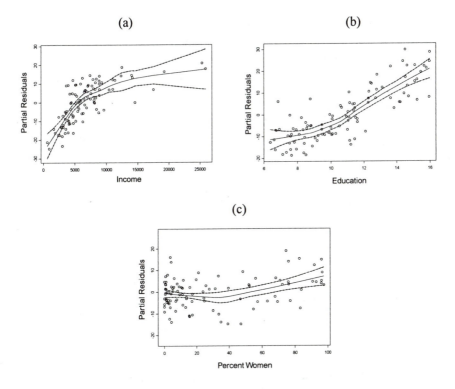

Figure 7.2. Estimated partial regression functions and partial residuals for the additive regression of prestige on income, education, and percent women. The broken lines give pointwise 95% confidence intervals around the fits. The additive model employs local linear least-squares smoothers with span = 0.6 for income and education and span = 0.8 for percent women.

quadratic relationship, employing terms in percent women and percent women squared. I invite the reader to fit this model to the data and to assess the adequacy of the result.

Another application of nonparametric regression analysis in support of traditional statistical modeling is in the analysis of residuals from regression models. If a model fit to the data is adequate, then the residuals should be unstructured—that is, unrelated to the predictors. Plotting residuals against individual predictors and smoothing the plot is a simple application of this point, but so is performing a more sophisticated nonparametric regression analysis of the residuals, such as a projection-pursuit regression[16]: If the residuals are unstructured, then the projection-pursuit regression should prove uninformative; structure in the residuals may suggest a modification of the model—for example, the incorporation of certain interactions among the predictors—or we may decide to abandon parametric modeling in favor of nonparametric regression.

Linear and generalized linear models are mature methodologies at the heart of statistical data analysis in the social sciences. It would be premature and foolish to suggest the wholesale replacement of these models with nonparametric regression. But linear and generalized linear models make strong assumptions about the structure of data—in particular, an assumption of linearity—that are generally unwarranted by the research questions, hypotheses, and social theory that motivate data analysis. It is therefore equally foolish to suggest that these methods should be applied to data blindly.

The status attainment literature, for example, of which Blishen and McRoberts's (1976) work on the prestige of Canadian occupations is an instance, is motivated by a Weberian perspective on social differentiation and inequality. This perspective leads Blishen and McRoberts to expect that prestige should rise with the income and educational levels of occupations, but they have no prior reason to believe that the relationship between prestige and these predictors is linear. There is no advantage to blindly assuming a linear relationship—unless, of course, the assumption is correct, and how are we to know without looking? Even in the rare instance that theory suggests a linear relationship, it is only sensible to find out if the data bear out this expectation. An accurate description of the data is a necessary ingredient of effective statistical analysis.

Although it is, as I said, premature to advocate the abandonment of parametric statistical models, I expect that nonparametric modeling, and other computationally intensive statistical procedures, will gradually become more common as computers and computational methods continue to improve. These methods have much to offer the practicing data analyst.

NOTES

1. The performance of smoothing splines and local polynomial regression can be improved by locally varying the smoothness of these estimators according to the roughness of the regression function—for example, by adjusting the bandwidth of the local-polynomial estimator (as discussed, e.g., in Fox, 2000, Section 4.3).

2. "Lowess" (Cleveland, 1979) stands for "*lo*cally *we*ighted *s*catterplot *s*moother" and applies only to simple regression; the more recent acronym "loess" (Cleveland, Grosse, and Shyu, 1992) stands for "*lo*cal regre*ss*ion" and is more general.

3. The predictors in Figure 2.2(a) are standardized for comparability with the other parts of the figure (see below). Standardization does not affect the product marginal weights.

4. The heuristic here is as follows: In product marginal kernel weighting of uniformly distributed data, marginal spans of 0.7 produce a neighborhood including roughly half of the data (recall Section 2.2).

5. As explained in Section 2.1, a (potentially asymmetric) nearest-neighbor estimator such as loess includes in each local fit the $m = [sn]$ observations with x values closest to the focal x_0. A symmetric nearest-neighbor estimator ensures that $m/2$ observations are on either side of the focal value; therefore, m has to grow smaller as the boundaries of the data are approached. The details of the supersmoother are intricate and may be found in Härdle (1990, pp. 181–184) or Hastie and Tibshirani (1990, pp. 70–71). Friedman's original 1984 paper proposing the supersmoother is available only as a technical report. Here, however, is an outline of the method:

- At each x_i, local linear fits are computed for $m = 0.05n$, $0.2n$, and $0.5n$ observations, omitting the focal value from the fits, to get cross-validated residuals.
- The squared residuals are themselves smoothed over the x values, and a preliminary optimal span is selected at each x_i.
- The preliminary optimal spans are then smoothed over the x values and used to compute the smooth $\widehat{y}_i$.

6. A better approach here would be to compute an incremental F test for the second projection, but to do so requires approximate degrees of freedom for the models. In principle, calculating degrees of freedom is not difficult (see below), but the software employed for this example, Friedman and Stuetzle's "ppreg" function in S-Plus, does not report degrees of freedom.

7. Although this result is appealing in its simplicity, it is arguably better here to standardize the predictors by their interquartile ranges, rather than by their standard deviations, because income is substantially positively skewed. Doing so produces coefficients of 2.21 for standardized income and 4.20 for standardized education.

8. It is typical to require that each node produced by a split contain no fewer than, say, five observations; if there are no ties, then the number of splits to consider is reduced to $n - 9$.

9. Fitted values are obtained by "sending" an observation through the tree to a leaf, at each node choosing one branch according to the value of the corresponding predictor for that observation. This is a straightforward process for quantitative predictors, because it is always possible to decide whether the current x is above or below a cutoff. When there are categorical predictors, however, complications can arise, because the current x may not correspond to either branch. A solution is to assign as a fitted value the mean response at the interior node where this anomaly arises.

10. The "boundary bias" of kernel estimates refers to the artificial flattening of the regression curve that occurs near the edges of the data. See Fox (2000, Sections 3 and 4.2).

11. There are complications here: The pseudo-response is itself a function of the fitted values,

$$z_i = \widehat{\eta}_i + \frac{y_i - \widehat{\mu}_i}{\widehat{\mu}_i(1 - \widehat{\mu}_i)},$$

and, unlike in the additive regression model, the coefficients r_{ij} for transforming the pseudo-response depend upon the observed y_i's. The results given here hold aymptotically, however. See Hastie and Tibshirani (1990, Section 6.8.2).

12. Long also includes the log of the wife's estimated wage rate as a predictor, but because of the problematic definition of this variable (see Section 6.1), I excluded it. The table of predictors is repeated from Section 1.1.

13. For these data, I was unable to obtain results from 10-fold cross-validation, as the "cv.tree" function in S-plus failed consistently, and some custom programming was required to get five-fold cross-validation to work properly.

14. These sources also discuss alternatives to traditional partial residual plots that perform better under these circumstances.

15. Selection of linearizing transformations by visual trial and error is discussed in Fox (2000, Section 6.1). It is also possible to select transformations in regression analytically by formally estimating the transformations as parameters (see, e.g., Fox, 1997, Section 12.5). In this instance, both approaches produce essentially the same result: the log of income and the square of education.

16. I am grateful to Robert Stine, of the University of Pennsylvania, for suggesting this application of projection-pursuit regression to me. Friedman and Stuetzle (1981, p. 819) also make this point in passing.

REFERENCES

ALDRICH, J. H., and NELSON, F. D. (1984). *Linear Probability, Logit, and Probit Models* (Sage University Paper series on Quantitative Applications in the Social Sciences, series no. 07-45). Beverly Hills, CA: Sage.

BERNDT, E. R. (1991). *The Practice of Econometrics: Classic and Contemporary.* Reading, MA: Addison-Wesley.

BLISHEN, B. R., and MCROBERTS, H. A. (1976). A revised socioeconomic index for occupations in Canada. *Canadian Review of Sociology and Anthropology*, 13, 71–79.

BLOOMFIELD, P. (1976). *Fourier Analysis of Time Series: An Introduction.* New York: Wiley.

BOWMAN, A. W., and AZZALINI, A. (1997). *Applied Smoothing Techniques for Data Analysis: The Kernel Approach with S-Plus Illustrations.* Oxford, UK: Oxford University Press.

BREIMAN, L., and FRIEDMAN, J. H. (1985). Estimating optimal transformations for multiple regression and correlation (with discussion). *Journal of the American Statistical Association*, 80, 580–619.

BREIMAN, L., FRIEDMAN, J. H., OLSHEN, R. A., and STONE, C. J. (1984). *Classification and Regression Trees.* Belmont, CA: Wadsworth.

CLARK, L. A., and PREGIBON, D. (1992). Tree-based models. In J. M. Chambers and T. J. Hastie (Eds.), *Statistical Models in S* (pp. 377–419). Pacific Grove, CA: Wadsworth and Brooks/Cole.

CLEVELAND, W. S. (1979). Robust locally weighted regression and smoothing scatterplots. *Journal of the American Statistical Association*, 74, 829–836.

CLEVELAND, W. S. (1993). *Visualizing Data.* Summit, NJ: Hobart Press.

CLEVELAND, W. S., GROSSE, E., and SHYU, W. M. (1992). Local regression models. In J. M. Chambers and T. J. Hastie (Eds.), *Statistical Models in S* (pp. 309–376). Pacific Grove, CA: Wadsworth and Brooks/Cole.

COOK, R. D. (1998). *Regression Graphics: Ideas for Studying Regressions Through Graphics.* New York: Wiley.

COOK, R. D., and WEISBERG, S. (1999). *Applied Regression Including Computing and Graphics.* New York: Wiley.

EINHORN, H. J. (1972). Alchemy in the behavioral sciences. *Public Opinion Quarterly*, 36, 367–378.

ELIASON, S. R. (1993). *Maximum Likelihood Estimation: Logic and Practice* (Sage University Paper Series on Quantitative Applications in the Social Sciences, series no. 07-096). Newbury Park, CA: Sage.

FAN, J., and GIJBELS, I. (1996). *Local Polynomial Modelling and Its Applications.* London: Chapman and Hall.

FOX, J. (1991). *Regression Diagnostics* (Sage University Paper series on Quantitative Applications in the Social Sciences, series no. 07-79). Newbury Park, CA: Sage.

FOX, J. (1997). *Applied Regression Analysis, Linear Models, and Related Methods.* Thousand Oaks, CA: Sage.

82

FOX, J. (2000). *Nonparametric Simple Regression: Smoothing Scatterplots* (Sage University Paper series on Quantitative Applications in the Social Sciences, series no. 07-130). Thousand Oaks, CA: Sage.

FRIEDMAN, J. H., and STUETZLE, W. (1981). Projection pursuit regression. *Journal of the American Statistical Association*, 76, 817–823.

HÄRDLE, W. (1990). *Applied Nonparametric Regression*. Cambridge, UK: Cambridge University Press.

HÄRDLE, W. (1991). *Smoothing Techniques with Implementation in S*. New York: Springer-Verlag.

HASTIE, T. J. (1992). Generalized additive models. In J. M. Chambers and T. J. Hastie, (Eds.), *Statistical Models in S* (pp. 249–307). Pacific Grove, CA: Wadsworth and Brooks/Cole.

HASTIE, T. J., and TIBSHIRANI, R. J. (1990). *Generalized Additive Models*. London: Chapman and Hall.

JACOBY, W. G. (1998). *Statistical Graphics for Visualizing Multivariate Data* (Sage University Paper series on Quantitative Applications in the Social Sciences, series no. 07-120). Thousand Oaks, CA: Sage.

LONG, J. S. (1997). *Regression Models for Categorical and Limited Dependent Variables*. Thousand Oaks, CA: Sage.

MCCULLAGH, P., and NELDER, J. A. (1989). *Generalized Linear Models* (2nd ed.). London: Chapman and Hall.

MENARD, S. (1995). *Applied Logistic Regression Analysis* (Sage University Paper series on Quantitative Applications in the Social Sciences, series no. 07-106). Thousand Oaks, CA: Sage.

MORGAN, J. N., and MESSENGER, R. C. (1973). *THAID: A Sequential Search Program for the Analysis of Nominal Scale Dependent Variables*. University of Michigan, Ann Arbor: Institute for Social Research.

MROZ, T. A. (1987). The sensitivity of an empirical model of married women's hours of work to economic and statistical assumptions. *Econometrica*, 55, 765–799.

NASON, G. P., and SILVERMAN, B. W. (1994). The discrete wavelet transform in S. *Journal of Computational and Graphical Statistics*, 3, 163–191.

NASON, G. P., and SILVERMAN, B. W. (in press). Wavelets for regression and other statistical problems. In M. G. Schimek (Ed.), *Smoothing and Regression: Approaches, Computation, and Application*. New York: Wiley.

SIMONOFF, J. S. (1996). *Smoothing Methods in Statistics*. New York: Springer-Verlag.

SONQUIST, J. A., and MORGAN, J. N. (1964). *The Detection of Interaction Effects*. University of Michigan, Ann Arbor: Institute for Social Research.

TIBSHIRANI, R. (1988). Estimating transformations for regression via additivity and variance stabilization. *Journal of the American Statistical Association*, 83, 394–405.

VENABLES, W. N., AND RIPLEY, B. D. (1997). *Modern Applied Statistics with S-PLUS*. (2nd ed.). New York: Springer-Verlag.

ABOUT THE AUTHOR

John Fox is Professor of Sociology at McMaster University in Hamilton, Ontario, Canada. He has written and lectured widely on social statistics. Professor Fox is the author of an earlier monograph on *Regression Diagnostics* (Sage, 1991) in the QASS series and of *Applied Regression Analysis, Linear Models, and Related Methods* (Sage, 1997). He is also the author of the companion QASS monograph, *Nonparametric Simple Regression: Smoothing Scatterplots* (Sage, 2000). His recent and current research includes work on polls in the 1995 Quebec sovereignty referendum and the 1997 Canadian federal election, and experiments on the perception of three-dimensional dynamic statistical graphs.

Quantitative Applications in the Social Sci̶

A SAGE UNIVERSITY PAPERS SERIES

Other volumes in this series listed on outside back cover

Quantitative Applications in the Social Sciences

A SAGE UNIVERSITY PAPERS SERIES

Visit our website at www.sagepub.co

ISBN 0-7619-2189-3

9 780761 921899

90000

SAGE PUBLICATIONS
International Educational and Professional Publisher
Thousand Oaks   London   New Delhi

P8-CTD-944